BECOME SMARTER EVERY DAY

AVIRAL PATHAK

India was the mother of our race and Sanskrit the mother of Europe's languages. She was the mother of our philosophy, mother through the Arabs, of much of our mathematics, mother through Buddha, of the ideals embodied in Christianity, mother through village communities of self-government and democracy. Mother India is in many ways the mother of us all.

-Aviral Pathak

Contents

Foreword

21 chapter to learn

Preface

TO BECOME SMARTER EVERY DAY

I Am Aviral Pathak Co-Founder Of Open Box Want To Tell My Readers This Book Is Worth It

Acknowledgements

How We Learn To Read

I bet you already know how to read a book. You were taught in elementary school.

But do you know how to read well?

There is a difference between reading for understanding and reading for information.

If you're like most people, you probably haven't given much thought to how you read. And how you read makes a massive difference to knowledge accumulation.

A lot of people confuse knowing the name of something with understanding. While great for exercising your memory, the regurgitation of facts without solid understanding and context gains you little in the real world.

A useful heuristic: Anything easily digested is reading for information.

Consider the newspaper, are you truly learning anything new? Do you consider the writer your superior when it comes to knowledge in the subject? Odds are probably not. That means you're reading for information. It means you're likely to parrot an opinion that isn't yours as if you had done the work.

This is how most people read. But most people aren't really learning anything new. It's not going to give you an edge, make you better at your job, or allow you to avoid problems.

"Marking a book is literally an experience of your differences or agreements with the author. It is the highest respect you can pay him."

— Edgar Allen Poe

Learning something insightful requires mental work. It's uncomfortable. If it doesn't hurt, you're not learning. You need to find writers who are more knowledgeable on a particular subject than yourself. By narrowing the gap between the author and yourself, you get smarter.

The Four Levels of Reading

Mortimer Adler literally wrote the book on reading. Adler identifies four levels of reading:

Elementary Reading

Inspectional Reading

Analytical Reading

Syntopical Reading

How You Read Matches Why You're Reading

The goal of reading determines how you read. Reading the latest Danielle Steel novel is not the same as reading Plato. If you're reading for entertainment or information, you're going to read a lot differently (and likely different material) than reading to increase understanding. While many people are proficient in reading for information and entertainment, few improve their ability to read for knowledge.

Before we can improve our reading skills, we need to understand the differences in the reading levels. They are thought of as levels because you can't move to a higher level without a firm understanding of the previous one — they are cumulative.

1. Elementary Reading

This is the level of reading taught in our elementary schools. If you're reading this website, you already know how to do this.

2. Inspectional Reading

We've been taught that skimming and superficial reading are bad for understanding. That is not necessarily the case. Using these tools effectively can increase understanding. Inspectional reading allows us to look at the author's blueprint and evaluate the merits of a deeper reading experience.

There are two sub-types of inspectional reading:

Systematic skimming — This is meant to be a quick check of the book by (1) reading the preface; (2) studying the table of contents; (3) checking the index; and (4) reading the inside jacket. This should give you sufficient knowledge to understand the chapters in the book, pivotal to the author's argument. Dip in here and there, but never with more than a paragraph or two. Skimming helps you reach to a decision point: Does this book deserve more of my time and attention? If not, you put it down.

Superficial reading — This is when you just read. Don't ponder the argument, don't look things up, don't write in the margins. If you don't understand something, move on. What you gain from this quick read will help you later when you go back and put more effort into reading. You now come to another decision point. Now that you have a better understanding of the book's contents and its structure, do you want to understand it?

Inspectional reading gives you the gist of things.

Sometimes that's all we want or need. But sometimes we want more. Sometimes we want to understand.

Read more about Inspectional Reading.

3. Analytical Reading

Francis Bacon once remarked, "some books are to be tasted, others to be swallowed, and some few to be chewed and digested."

You can think of analytical reading as doing that chewing and digesting. This is doing the work.

Analytical reading is a thorough reading.

If inspectional reading is the best you can do quickly, this is the best reading you can do given time.

At this point, you start to engage your mind and dig into the work required to understand what's being said. I highly recommend you use marginalia to converse with the author.

There are four rules to Analytical Reading

Classify the book according to kind and subject matter.

State what the whole book is about with the utmost brevity.

Enumerate its major parts in their order and relation, and outline these parts as you have outlined the whole.

Define the problem or problems the author is trying to solve.

You'll probably notice that while those sound pretty easy, they involve a lot of work. Luckily the inspectional reading you've already done has primed you for this.

After an inspectional read, you will understand the book and the author's views.

But that doesn't mean you'll understand the broader subject. To do that, you need to use comparative reading to synthesize knowledge from several books on the same subject.

Read More About Analytical Reading.

4. Syntopical Reading

This is also known as comparative reading, and it represents the most demanding and difficult reading of all. Syntopical Reading involves reading many books on the same subject and comparing and contrasting ideas, vocabulary, and arguments.

This task is undertaken by identifying relevant passages, translating the terminology, framing and ordering the questions that need answering, defining the issues, and having a conversation with the responses.

The goal is not to achieve an overall understanding of any particular book, but rather to understand the subject and develop a deep fluency.

This is all about identifying and filling in your knowledge gaps.

There are five steps to syntopical reading:

Finding the Relevant Passages — You need to find the right books and then the passages that are most relevant to filling your needs. So the first step is an inspectional reading of all the works that you have identified as relevant.

Bringing the Author to Terms — In analytical reading, you must identify the keywords and how they are used by the author. This is fairly straightforward. The process becomes more complicated now as each author has probably used different terms and concepts to frame their argument. Now the onus is on you to establish the terms. Rather than using the author's language, you must use your own. In short, this is an exercise in translation and synthesis.

Getting the Questions Clear — Rather than focus on the problems the author is trying to solve, you need to focus on the questions that you want answered. Just as we must establish our own terminology, so too must we establish our own propositions by shedding light on our problems to which the authors provide answers. It's important to frame the questions in such a way that all or most of the authors can be interpreted as providing answers. Sometimes we might not get an answer to our questions because they might not have been seen as questions by the authors.

Defining the Issues — If you've asked a clear question to which there are multiple answers then an issue has been defined. Opposing answers, now translated into your terms, must be ordered in relation to one another. Understanding multiple perspectives within an issue helps you form an intelligent opinion.

Analyzing the Discussion — It's presumptuous to expect we'll find a single unchallenged truth to any of our questions. Our answer is the conflict of opposing answers. The value is the discussion you have with these authors. You can now have an informed opinion.

Becoming a Demanding Reader

Reading is all about asking the right questions in the right order and seeking answers.

There are four main questions you need to ask of every book:

What is this book about?

What is being said in detail, and how?

Is this book true in whole or in part?

What of it?

ONE

5 Brilliant Tips: How To Become Smarter Every Day

Constant personal growth is vital if you are not willing to be left behind. The contemporary world forces us to move as fast as never before. It seems like the velocity is extremely high and there is no time to hit a pause and take a breath.

As a result, we are provided with such a great variety of information that we have to improve our knowledge and skills to process it and stay up-to-date. Otherwise, we risk being outpaced and eventually ending up falling behind the progress.

We live in the epoch where there is a growing demand for people who possess idiosyncratic knowledge and skills. Being smart is a trend. Being smart is crucial if you want to fit this fast growing world.

However, being smart is a temporary state unless you maintain it regularly.

Here are 5 tips to help become smarter every day:

1. Become Obsessed.

The obsession in a good sense is the most powerful tool that is going to lead you to the desired destination. You need to become obsessed with the idea of being smart. Make it your primary objective, but not the secondary option. When you are dedicated to the idea, you are no longer looking for excuses and do not do anything that does not add any value to the achievement of your goals. Meanwhile, you commit to your ambitions and move gradually towards their accomplishments.

2. Do Not Let Yourself Grow Up.

Stay curious and interested in everything that surrounds you. Be open-minded and absorb new knowledge as you were a child. With age people adopt an idea that they know everything and there is no need to learn anything new. This mindset is not going to make you smarter. Do not stop studying and always stay hungry for knowledge. Explore the world and discover earlier unknown things for you. Learn to ask smart questions and demand exhaustive answers.

3. Become Friends With Books

It is difficult to overestimate how powerful the plain old-fashioned reading is. It is exciting. It is interesting. It is simply a great exercise for your brain and a means of studying. Develop a habit to always have a book with you. Then you will not waste any moment standing in a queue or waiting for a bus, but rather convert every minute into the effective process of broadening your knowledge. Challenge yourself to read one book every week and try to stick to this schedule. Read. Read a lot.

4. Surround Yourself With The Smart

It is impossible to improve your knowledge if you are still the smartest guy in a room. Make sure you grow in the environment where you always feel that you lack skills and knowledge. You need to feel a pressure and at the same time a motivation to fill the gaps in your experience. Keep away from people who do not inspire you for greater results and never challenge you to become better. Get around people who can share their unique expertise, teach you new things and help you broaden your knowledge in the fields you are interested in.

5. Become More Observant

Learn from those who surround you. Look around. There are tons of examples, ideas, words, wisdom, mistakes, and experiences. Develop a habit to pay attention to details, analyze them and learn something new from each of them. The world consists of tiny things that are worth your attention. There are much more sources of knowledge than you think. You just have to notice them. Become more observant and attentive. Absorb knowledge from everywhere. Listen to others and try to extract as much valuable information as possible from every single situation.

Being smart is not a constant state. It is a constant process of self-improvement. Being smart is not a trait. It is a lifestyle. Being smart is an approach to everyday issues that is aimed at consistent acquirement of new knowledge and skills.

TWO

HOW TO LEARN FASTER IF YOU ARE NOT A GENIUS

Simple tools to learn any skill faster.

By improving their learning speed, some people achieved seemingly impossible feats. One student finished the MIT computer science curriculum in one year instead of four. Another learned nine languages while touring Europe.

The crazy thing is these super learners are not born like this — they learn to learn faster as you would any other skill. Yes, you can boost your learning speed.

Finishing college in a year and speaking nine languages are extreme cases. Yet, boosting your learning speed, even by little, grants you huge long term benefits.

If you learn to learn faster, your career or business grows quicker than others; you outsmart your competitors and even rank at the top of tournaments.

How can you learn faster? It has to do with a method called meta-learning. Let me explain.

A technique to help you learn anything faster

Here's the thing: whatever you want to learn, don't just pick a course and dive straight into it — most curricula, whether online or in school, aren't optimised for your personal needs.

You must build a learning map that helps you reach the outcome you want as fast as possible. This technique of building learning maps is known as meta-learning.

Scott Young discusses meta-learning in his book: Ultralearning. Many famous entrepreneurs, such as Elon Musk and Gabriel Weinberg, use it.

To give you an example, imagine you must empty a hundred water bottles as fast as you can. If you don't know the trick of fast discharge (swirling the bottle), you'll do what most people do — flip the bottle into the sink and squeeze it — a massive waste of time.

Meta-learning is like the trick to empty a water bottle faster — it's all about the methods that can help you speed up your learning.

Here's a three-step strategy to build learning maps that will help you learn any topic super fast.

1 — Know your type of motivation to learn

When you learn something new, your motivation is either internal or external.

Internal motivation: you learn because you genuinely enjoy the topic; you have a passion for it. For example, you want to speak French because you love how it sounds.

External motivation: you learn to achieve a specific outcome not related to the topic you want to learn. For example, you want to learn software, writing, or entrepreneurship, to make a lot of money.

Here's your first step: Know which kind of motivation drives you to learn.

Why? Because a topic has many sections, and most of them are irrelevant to your goal.

Once you have a clear image of the outcome you want, focus your time and energy on the best sections and skip the trivials forever or later.

2 — Build the structure before you start

Learning a skill is like navigating a building to look for a treasure.

If you know the structure of a building better than everyone, you'll take the fastest route to get what you want inside that building.

Here's your second step: Learn the structure of the topic to speed up your understanding.

To do so, create a table with three columns: concepts, facts, and procedures.

Concepts are the things you need to understand the topic. They are the fundamental principles, theories, and formalisms.

Facts are truthful things that you must know and remember about the topic. They come in the form of laws, techniques, or statements.

Procedures are all the actions you must take to get better at the topic. They increase your skill level and practical knowledge.

1 — Find all possible concepts, facts, and procedures and write them down.

2 — Order the items from each column by the level of challenge and importance — give an impact factor to each item.

3 — Gather the resources relevant to each concept, fact, and procedure.

Once you finish, you'll have a good knowledge tree for the topic. You'll understand the obstacles you will face and the best ways to overcome them.

"It is important to view knowledge as a tree. Make sure you understand the fundamental principles (the trunk and big branches) before you get into the leaves (details) or there is nothing for them to hang on to."

— Elon Musk

3 — Know where to start and what to leave

Knowing where to start and what to leave later will make a massive difference to your learning speed. The B.E.E (Benchmark, Emphasis, and Exclude) method will help you do that. This brings you to the third step.

Benchmark

Gather highly rated resources — best selling online courses, books, articles, and top university courses.

Download the syllabus of the resources you gathered.

Look for common patterns in these syllabi.

Focus on areas with maximum overlap.

Emphasise and Exclude

To reach the desired level of mastery as soon as possible, you must customise your curriculum to fit your personal goal.

The way to achieve this is by maintaining what is important to you and excluding what is not. Here are two examples:

If you want to speak Italian during a trip to Florence, emphasise learning to pronounce and exclude learning how to spell.

If you want to build apps quickly, focus on app development rather than theories of computer science.

Take Away

Super learning is not talent or genius-linked; it's a skill you can learn to increase your learning speed greatly.

A sure path to being a super learner is to use meta-learning. Build learning maps to help you understand the sections of your topic faster than ordinary people.

No matter what field you dream of mastering, meta-learning will speed your learning compared to your workmates and competitors. And the more you use meta-learning, the more efficient you become at learning — it's a certain way for you to become a super learner.

THREE

8 Habits of Successful People

it will turn your life upside down

Do you wonder why some reach sky-high heights, while others walk all their lives with their heads down to the ground? Maybe millionaires are born wearing dollar shirts, while top businessmen get everything on a silver platter? Do you believe in this yourself?

The path to success is long, thorny and often requires sacrifice.

Brian Tracy said:

If you want to have what you never had, become what you never had. Fortunately, we have learned how to do it.

1. Give your maximum

Of course, if the ultimate dream is to work as a cashier in a supermarket, you can not really strain. But if you want more, you have to sweat. And the higher the bar, the more strength you need to jump to it.

Is it logical? Quite, but many want to get everything at once, but do not change their lifestyle and habits. Get a job at Microsoft with only a free online coding course behind you. Or immediately become a boss, command others and receive 100,500 money.

But that doesn't happen – you have to give it your all first. How much? Grant Cardon came up with a universal rule: 10 times more than now.

2. Correctly formulate goals

I want to become rich - not a goal, but a daring request to the Universe. I want to make a million - better, but still not very good. Why did you surrender such money, where will you get it, how much time will you spend to accumulate the desired amount?

The correct formulation begins with the search for answers to the questions: why, how, why. Try to use such a scheme and be sure to connect each item with yourself: why am I doing this, how will I achieve what I want, what will I do with it later.

Analyze the origins of desire, formulate an adequate goal and work out ways to achieve it. To get started, you can perform a simple exercise: take any "Wishlist" and find your "Why" in it.

3. Take responsibility

image by @aviral_pathak_

Do you know how natural-born leaders differ from "average" ones? They are not afraid to take personal responsibility. People who are used to hiding their heads in the sand at the first stress or blaming everything on others (colleagues, boss, government, reptilians) are doomed to lose. All that remains for them is to be content with little and treat neuroses. And they will definitely arise if every day you torment yourself with anxious thoughts like "What if they ask me?".

Will definitely ask. Your task is to learn how to answer. And sometimes even risk your own skin and take on difficult challenges.

4. Manage your time wisely

Do you think you need to throw everything on the altar of work, hide from the world and count every minute spent outside the office as lost? In vain. Familiar to economists and businessmen, the Pareto law says: 80% of the result is achieved at the expense of 20% of the resources. Of the 100 employees of the company, only 20 move the business. Not the whole team knocks out the victory in the match, but the "productive" backbone — 20% of the composition. If you work 10 hours a day, your main activity only takes 2. How to plan time correctly? Bring the 80/20 principle to automatism and remember that the KKD of time is always 20%.

5. CLEAR PRIORITIES

Vital, personal, situational. You should be doing really important things, and not wasting 100% of your time on nonsense. The secret of successful people is simple - they do not lose efficiency, because they do not scatter their strength and motivation on everything.

If you often scroll through the thought "Again the day has passed, and nothing has been done" and transfer a bunch of things to tomorrow, next month or after a rain on Thursday, everything is very bad. There is only one way out - to quickly learn to focus on the main thing.

6. BE ABLE TO WORK IN A TEAM

Be able to work in a team To interact with others, losers use different strategies:

⊙ Consider everyone as enemies, move away and constantly wait for a catch;

⊙ They are afraid of judgment and every day strengthen the fence around their own comfort zone (which for some reason is narrowing all the time);

⊙ Consider themselves an empty place and try to "fill up" at the expense of others;

⊙ They think that everyone around them owes them, and they are indignant that no one is in a hurry to fulfill their wishes.

Such strategies have a lot in common - they are stupid, pointless and fail. Instead of competition, rejection of criticism and aggression, successful people choose cooperation, joint development and goodwill. They respect themselves and others, are willing to compromise and know the limits of their own competencies. Because they understood long ago: to achieve success together with those who are nearby is much easier, more pleasant and faster than alone.

7. LEARN FROM OTHERS

They say you need to learn from your mistakes. But people have a tendency to quickly forget failures and dance on a rake for a long time. Often mistakes only help to fill new bumps.

If you have a specific goal, you should look at those who have already achieved it. Millionaires from the Forbes list, businessmen, investors, entrepreneurs, startups are ideal role models, excellent advisers and a storehouse of valuable information.

8. LOOK IN DIFFERENT WAYS

For many years, a curious trend has been observed in the world. The rich and famous travel, do charity work, lead an active lifestyle, read and socialize a lot. Office workers, aspiring entrepreneurs, and freelancers are obsessed with work and see nothing else.

Walking around, hanging out at a bar with friends, watching a movie, reading a book, cuddling a cat doesn't mean losing efficiency. These are the things that make life better and the road to the goal enjoyable.

Try to dilute complex adult affairs with simple children's joys. And let's see what we have come to.

You will do it!

Just keep up the good work!

FOUR

8 HABITS FOR YOUR 20S

The 20s is that stage of life where we need to take our decisions wisely. So today I'll share 8 Habits that you should take up in your 20s.

Habits are something that can take you far in life because if you set goals and targets, then it is not necessary that you hit them, and if you don't hit them then you abuse and curse yourself. But if you hit them, you feel like a king. But there is no basis for us to set those goals and targets in the first place. I believe that most of the goals and targets we set for ourselves are nothing but our desires. Instead, if you focus on Habits then you can succeed far more.

Habit 1: Call People by their name

Whenever you write an E-mail or a message, please don't write, "Hi Bro", "Hey Bro" and so on. You have to write the name of that person. When you do that you create an emotional bond. People realize that you know their name, remember their name, and they feel familiar with the most precious thing we have, Our Name.

Habit 2: Write Emails to yourself in the Future

If you come across something that you want to do, let's say, an idea for a new article struck me, but I know that it is not the right time to write that article, so I will draft an email for myself, write the whole idea down, then I will set or schedule that email for that time when I can write that article, it could be after 3 months or 6 months later. What you do by this is that you set yourself to milestones. This is not a goal or target, it is a reflection. It says that does not increase your to-do list by this thing or remembering this thing right now, I will do it when it is the right time. But when you get into the habit of sending emails to yourself in the future, you basically are planning your future in a small way but in a meaningful way.

Habit 3: Do not try and remember everything

Everything on paper, everything on the calendar, everything on the Notes app, everything should be documented. We waste so much of our brain is just trying to remember things. The function of the mind is not to remember things, the function of the mind is to DO things. So you have to spend your mind and your energy in getting things done, not in remembering things. You can document everything using pen and paper, so you don't have to remember anything.

Habit 4: Wake up and smile at the mirror

Every day when you wake up, stand in front of the mirror and smile at yourself. Because if you will not love yourself, then no one else will love you. If you will be not kind to yourself, then nobody else will be kind to you. You have to become your biggest supporter, and this habit can take you so far ahead when you are always kind towards yourself. You stand in front of the mirror, no matter how bad the time maybe, even if you feel bad about yourself, you will smile and acknowledge that you exist.

Habit 5: Meet someone new every week

Every week meet someone you have never met. And it could be, a virtual interaction, it could be a physical or in-person interaction, that doesn't matter. It could be a very meaningful interaction where you are trying to know them or you want to learn something from them, or it could be just a nice happy just getting-to-know-them conversation. That doesn't matter. The key is that you are meeting new people every week, not to form meaningful relationships, but just to understand perspectives.

Habit 6: Read 30 minutes every day

I know it is tough but I am sharing this with you with a little twist. You have to read every day for 30 mins only, not towards any goal or target, you don't have to finish a book within a week or a month or a year, all you have to do is just read every day for 30 minutes.

Habit 7: Say thank you even if they're not listening

Having gratitude or being grateful is a very important skill in life. We often start taking people for granted. When people do something for us, we often tell ourselves, 'This was normal, anybody could do it. Anyone in their place could do it.' But that is not how you want to live life. You have to form a habit, as soon as possible in life, that ' I will have to acknowledge every person who does something for me.' And it has to be felt. You want to be grateful! You genuinely want to say thank you to people.

Habit 8: Don't leave inspiration to chance

You will have to form a habit where you are not dependent on luck to be inspired. For Example, you watch a motivational video, you get goosebumps. You get inspired, you get motivated, and you do something! How did this happen ? Did it happen because YouTube algorithm presented that video to you? Or did that happen because you actually went looking for something to inspire you? The second is what you want to do. You will have to do something every day in your life that inspires you. Whether it is a video, writing, a song, a dance, a sport, anything that leaves you high on energy, high on motivation, high on inspiration because it is your responsibility to inspire yourself. You cannot leave that to an algorithm, you cannot leave that to luck, you cannot leave that to chance. Make inspiration a choice.

These are the 8 Habits for your 20s. Get started today. Which habits you are already involved in? How did it benefit your life? I would love to know all these in the comments section so that others get inspired from you, and hopefully start on their own habit schedule and journey.

FIVE

13 Signs You've Leveled-Up As a Person

According to meta-analytic data, confidence isn't what leads to success. Instead, successful behavior is what creates confidence.

Unlike dopamine which only lasts short-term, confidence is something you own, once you've earned it. Short-term pleasure and long-term joy are two fundamentally different outcomes.

Once you've begun succeeding at any endeavor, you'll reach a threshold where you must decide if you're ready to go to the next level. Most people get comfortable at a certain stage because they don't want to deal with the emotional purging involved in up-leveling.

When you decide to up-level and go bigger, your life becomes very difficult for a short period of time. You may have mastered algebra, but now you're in a calculus class and feel completely disoriented.

All of a sudden, the confidence you used to have feels completely gone. You're now wondering if you want to do this whole math thing... or whatever it is you're doing.

Despite having a firm foundation, you feel like you're standing on nothing, and that everything around you is falling apart.

Have you up-leveled lately? If so, this list of 13 will be familiar.

Don't fret, you've been through this before. You've come this far. You've battled hard. You've triumphed.

Now things are feeling rough. But it won't be long until you get your stride back. But this time, you'll be more evolved. More able. The stakes will be higher. You'll have more help and support. Everything will mean more.

Here's how you'll know if you've recently leveled up:

1. Your Confidence Temporarily Drops

"If you're freaked-out, that means you're a professional." — Shane Snow

If you've been successful in the past, and for some reason feel derailed, don't take that as a sign you're on the wrong path.

Chances are, you've up-leveled without realizing it. Said Dr. Stephen R. Covey, "We control our actions, but the consequences that flow from those actions are controlled by principles."

When you've mastered one set of principles, your life will improve. You'll become more competent, successful, and confident. Your interactions with other people will be far deeper and more meaningful. Your social group will shift from people solely interested in entertainment to people interested in solving problems and growth.

However, once you've mastered a certain level of principles, you'll become aware of and exposed to higher-order principles. Immediately, you'll feel like a child again. You don't know how these rules work. You'll begin making mistakes.

Your confidence will drop. People will say, "You don't seem like yourself."

You'll wonder if you'll ever be able to feel that same powerful feeling again. Don't worry, you will.

2. Everything Will Feel Like It's Falling Apart

Just before author Napoleon Hill's greatest success in life, he went through several months of depression.

Despite knowing deep within himself what he was capable of, he became paralyzed and incapable. He was at rock bottom. His life, finances, and relationships began falling apart.

Once the pain became severe enough, something happened. A switch flipped. He snapped. In his own words, "I was seized upon by my 'Other self'" which had zero fear, was completely clear, and operated with definiteness of purpose.

With this immediate clarity, he was able to get direct insights about how to achieve his goals. But this acceleration and advancement came after several months of failure, defeat, confusion, and depression. He had up-leveled and was facing bigger challenges and responsibilities than he ever had before. Said historian Will Durant, "I think the ability of the average man could be doubled if it were demanded, if the situation demanded."

It took a while for him to adapt to the higher-order demands of his new situation. But adapt he did. And adapt you will. You haven't yet risen as high as you're about to because you've never been demanded as much as you are now.

There's a fear of success lurking within you. You're not sure if you really want to keep ascending. But you already know within yourself that you will. You're resolved. It's done. You know it's happening. You're being pulled.

3. You'll Begin To Question Yourself and Your Goals

In the midst of your confusion and lack of performance — as your world is seemingly falling apart — you'll begin to question yourself and the path you're on.

First, your life isn't really falling apart. It's better now than it's ever been before. You're living at a much higher and more powerful level than ever before. You're just adjusting to what that means. You'll rise up.

But in the meantime, you'll question. Clarity will lack. You'll be surrounded by fog. You'll feel disoriented.

It's during these moments that you'll need to stick to your core practices for clarity. You'll need to deepen your learning, deepen your meditations/prayer. Even still, for a period of time, the clarity that once seemed to have an infinite flow will feel dried-up.

It will be very disheartening.

4. You'll Feel Alone — Even Among Close Friends

Despite developing deeper and better relationships — you'll feel alone. The alone time you need is necessary. At the same time, though, you need to maintain connection.

You're as sick as you're secrets.

Isolation won't help you get where you need to go. The more successful you become, the more connected you'll need to be. If you become isolated and stay isolated, you'll lose your mind. In that case, everything will permanently come crashing down. In the words of Greg McKeown, your "success will become a catalyst for failure."

So, take the time you need to get clarity. But be even more vulnerable and honest now with your "inner circle." You need them now more than ever. This doesn't mean you won't feel alone. You absolutely will feel alone. But just like the lack of confidence, this feeling will shortly go away. You're growing and be purged.

You'll soon see the people in your life with more love and gratitude than ever before. Your humility for all they do for you will peak. Your joy for the little things will surmount any achievement or goal you desire.

5. You'll Feel Numb To What Used To Inspire You

For a time, you'll feel totally disconnected from your passion, craft, and mission. What used to keep you awake at night with excitement now finds you sleeping-in in attempts to avoid.

The external pressure feels too much. It's harder to focus. It's harder to get into the zone. Harder to feel inspired. Harder to care.

This numbness isn't because you don't care, though. You've advanced in understanding. You've adapted. You're being double-teamed now. Your brain is being forced to deal with more at once. This is how you advance. This is how you develop deeper mastery and subconscious ability to perform even under the severest of conditions.

Seek the breakthroughs. They'll come. The light will break through. And soon enough, it will come through with more intensity than you've ever experienced before.

6. You'll Start Going Through The Motions and Continue to Succeed — But It Won't Be As Enjoyable

For a while, it will feel like you're going through the motions. You'll have so much momentum that muscle memory will take over. But your heart won't be in it for a short time.

You'll still succeed. But it won't matter to you, because you didn't push yourself. Succeeding will become boring because you're not in alignment with your why.

You're close, though, to reconnecting.

7. You'll Start Making Uncharacteristic Mistakes — And You Won't Be Bothered

With your temporary lack of confidence and stability, you'll begin dropping balls that were easy to hold before.

Small things that were once easy to figuratively lift will feel extremely heavy and difficult.

Initially, you'll be freaked out by the balls you're dropping. But at the same time, stability and sanity are more important. So you're willing to drop some pretty big balls.

To other people, the consequences seem impossibly big. But your mind has already been stretched. You have a much, much bigger vision. Although once big, these balls are now small in your mind. Your security is internal, so you know you'll be able to solve whatever problems may arise. To quote Josh Waitzin in The Art of Learning, "Sometimes limits need to be pushed."

8. Countless Opportunities Present Themselves — Distractions

"A 'once-in-a-lifetime opportunity' is irrelevant if it is the wrong opportunity." — Jim Collins

One of the problems with your situation is that more and more opportunities seem to be presenting themselves.

You leveled-up for a reason. You learned how to do things other people haven't discovered. You've developed what Cal Newport calls, "rare and valuable skills."

Your discernment will really need to sharpen if you're going to make it to the top of this level and up to the next. Most people "sell-out" at some point. The opportunities become too compelling and the vision fades into oblivion.

The only opportunities that matter are the one's that deeply resonate. Stay close to people you know deep down really care. There will be plenty of people out there who will tell you what they think you want to hear. And they'll be compelling... and you'll probably fall for it a time or two.

But don't buy it this time. The people you decide to maintain on your journey of life will determine your long-term success and inner-peace.

9. You'll Be Faced With A Crucial Decision

It's at this point that you're faced with the crucial decision — will you connect deeper with the WHY that brought you here? Or will you succumb to the pressure?

Pressure can busts pipes... or it can make diamonds.

Here is your moment. Your situation is poised. Everything you've done has brought you to this point. Now is your time to rise up or let up.

In order to reconnect with your WHY, you'll need to un-commit to several "opportunities" that were nothing more than appealing distractions. You'll need to have some hard conversations with the people who matter most. You'll need to get back to your core. You'll need to get back to the drawing board.

It's at this point that you can take all you've learned in the past and go bigger than you've ever gone before.

10. You'll Need to Adjust — What Got You Here Won't Get You There

The biggest fear of growth is the challenge that will be demanded. Now is your time to adjust to the newness. Embrace it.

Newness brings flow. It allows for more angles on the same beautiful experiences, relationships, and meanings you've had in the past.

11. You'll Need to Recommit — It Won't Be Easy, But It Will Come (You Can't Go Back)

"A mind that is stretched by a new experience can never go back to its old dimensions." — Oliver Wendell Holmes, Jr.

You need to get definitive again — like you were when you first caught fire. You'll need to get back to the beginner's mind. You'll need to want it bad enough to get extremely consistent again. No more lack of consistency. Now is the time to be more consistent than ever before.

12. You'll Quickly Adapt To Your New Lessons — Growth Will Come Shockingly Fast

Prepare for faster growth than you've ever experienced before. Your momentum is now multiplied and compounded.

You're no longer alone on your quest. You have lots of teammates and supporters who will help you. Not only that, but something inside of you expanded beyond the dimensions of what you could create. Now, you're creating, building, connecting, and living. It's a sight to see.

13. Enjoy It

Let it happen.

Enjoy it.

You're on to something great right now. Your confidence is back.

SIX

21 Behaviors That Will Make You Brilliant at Creativity & Relationship

————•♡•————

21 Behaviors That Will Make You Brilliant at Creativity & Relationships

When you see things from multiple perspectives, you realize you can achieve almost anything you want in far less time than you imagined.

Yet most people have fixed and limited views about themselves and what they can accomplish.

They have fixed and limited views about the resources available to them.

They have fixed and limited views about time, and how long things must take to accomplish.

In this article, I squash all of those limiting perspectives and provide concrete strategies you can use to achieve your goals. There are no fixed limits.

Here's how it works:

Core Principles

1. Set absurdly ambitious goals

"When 10x is your measuring stick, you immediately see how you can bypass what everyone else is doing." — Dan Sullivan

Goals are most likely to be accomplished when:

They are intrinsically motivating. As Napoleon Hill explained in Think and Grow Rich, "Desire is the starting point of all achievement, not a hope, not a wish, but a keen pulsating desire which transcends everything."

They must be difficult, or else they won't be motivating.

They must be time-bound, to create a sense of urgency. Shorter timelines are one way to go 10x, since they force you to shed artificial constraints and think more creatively. As billionaire Peter Thiel is known to ask: "How can you achieve your ten-year plan in the next six months?"

As with all things in life, you get what you want. If you prefer to make excuses and justifications for a lack of progress, then just admit you prefer your current station in life. Self-acceptance can be a beautiful thing.

However, once you desire progress more than convenience, obstacles no longer stop but propel you. As the Roman emperor Marcus Aurelius is famous for saying, "The impediment to action advances action. What stands in the way becomes the way."

2. Reframe subconscious patterns and get bold insights via auto-suggestion

"What is impressed in the subconscious is expressed." — Dr. Joseph Murphy in The Power of Your Subconscious Mind

While awake, your conscious and subconscious mind are often at odds with each other. For example, you're trying to be positive, but your subconscious patterns simply won't let you.

Yet, while transitioning from being awake to being asleep, your brain waves move from the active Beta state into Alpha and then Theta before eventually dropping into Delta as we sleep. It is during the Theta window that your mind is most receptive to reshaping your subconscious patterns. Hence, Thomas Edison is known for having said, "Never go to sleep without a request to your subconscious."

As a result, just before you fall asleep, it is key to visualize and even vocally state what you are trying to accomplish. When you repeatedly state a desired goal, visualization is key because you want to have as emotional an experience as possible. You need to feel what it would be like to have what you seek.

You can absolutely trust that by planting these subconscious seeds, thoughts will pop up at you, often at random intervals. You need to record these thoughts throughout your day. The bigger the goal, the bolder will be the required action to attain it. The clearer your why, the more inspired will be your how.

If you're serious, you'll need to act immediately upon the impressions your subconscious is transmitting to your conscious mind. If you brush off these insights, you'll get less and less of them. You'll demonstrate to yourself and the source of your inspiration that you don't really want the changes you claim to desire.

3. Learn and work in counterintuitive environments

1905 was Albert Einstein's breakthrough year where he published four research articles, known as the Annus Mirabilis papers, which went on to substantially alter the foundation of modern physics and changed views on space, time, and matter.

Interestingly, when Einstein published these papers, he was not working in an academic setting, but rather at the Swiss Patent Office. His work in this counterintuitive work environment allowed him different reflective angles and questions than a typical physics lab.

As Elon Musk's wife, Justine, has said:

"Choose one thing and become a master of it. Choose a second thing and become a master of that. When you become a master of two worlds (say, engineering and business), you can bring them together in a way that will a) introduce hot ideas to each other, so they can have idea sex and make idea babies that no one has seen before and b) create a competitive advantage because you can move between worlds, speak both languages, connect the tribes, mash the elements to spark fresh creative insight until you wake up with the epiphany that changes your life."

When you work in a different context from the majority of people in your field, you can make distinct and unique connections. You can integrate and cross-pollinate different ideas. You can avoid dogmatic thinking and expectations. You can learn to integrate ideas from seemingly dissimilar fields.

4. Learn from counterintuitive resources

"What does following in the footsteps of everyone else get you? It gets you to exactly the same conclusions as everyone else." — Ryan Holiday

As Holiday explains, if you read what everyone else is reading, you'll think like everyone else thinks. If you think like everyone else thinks, you won't be able to come up with anything unique.

Follow your curiosity. Chase down obscure leads. Find stuff that no one else has found. In this way, your work will be truly valuable to others.

5. Focus on the process (not results) of those who are succeeding big

"Success leaves clues." — Jim Rohn

Focusing exclusively on results is one of the primary reasons the current academic system is broken. Kids are being taught to train for the test, rather than seeking novel and unique ways of doing things. No two kids are wired the same, nor should their contribution, creativity, and talent be viewed from the same standard.

When you want to develop expertise at something, rather than focusing on the results of those at the top of your field, study and emulate their process.

What are they doing?

Once you get process-oriented, as opposed to results-oriented, you realize you too can achieve amazing results. The process, or your behavior, is completely within your control. Conversely, when you focus solely on other people's results, you can quickly become overwhelmed and give up.

6. Ignore what almost everyone else is doing

In the book Relentless: From Good to Great to Unstoppable, Tim Grover explains that the world's elite don't compete with other people. Rather, they make others compete with them. They set the tone and make others react to their environment.

Most people are competing with other people. They continuously check in to see what others in their space (their "competition") are doing. As a result, they mimic and copy what's "working."

Rather than worrying about what others are doing, live your values. Put first things first. Spend more time with your loved ones and away from work. While working, follow your own curiosity, not what others are doing.

7. 80/20 Analysis of highest leverage activities

"Today everyone is a generalist, a deliberate move on the part of most as a reaction to the economic times." — Leonard Smith

When studying the process of those you seek to emulate, don't try to do it all. Everyone has their own strategy. Even those at the top of your field have imperfect strategies.

Find the patterns. What are the key things you must master? Master those.

Then innovate beyond those patterns when you're ready, so your process comes to exceed the process of those you admire. Eventually, your results will exceed theirs as well.

8. Over-learn high leverage activities

Learning something new is all about memory and how you use it. At first, your prefrontal cortex — which stores your working (or short-term) memory — is really busy figuring out how the task is done.

But once you're proficient, the prefrontal cortex gets a break. In fact, it's freed up by as much as 90%. Once this happens, you can perform that skill automatically, leaving your conscious mind to focus on other things.

This level of performance is called automaticity, and reaching it depends on what psychologists call over-learning or over-training.

For example, if you want to quickly learn how to write viral articles, study several hundred headlines of viral articles. If you want to write a book, study just the table of contents of hundreds of books. These are your lay-ups.

Start with small sets of information, then expand from there. By over-learning a particular category of learning, you'll be able to better understand how it relates to the whole. You'll also quickly be able to apply what you learn. You'll quickly see the patterns others miss. Time will slow down for you as your cognition expands.

9. Learn to apply, not to procrastinate "the work"

"The key secret to success is not excessive expertise, but the ability to use it. Knowledge is worthless unless it is applied." — Max Lukominskyi

Learning is best done while you're doing the activity. Public education has taught people they must first master theory, then attempt to transfer that theory into the real world. In a similar way, people's love for information via the internet has led them to use "learning" as a form of procrastination.

A better approach is "context-based learning," where you learn while doing. The key principles of context-based learning include:

Learn a concept in its simplest form.

Put your rudimentary knowledge to practice in a real-world scenario.

Get coaching and feedback (feedback often comes in the form of "failure").

Apply the feedback through repetitious practice.

Get coaching and feedback.

Repeat until proficient (see #8 just above).

Interestingly, researchers examined the effects of role-playing on the self-concept of shy adolescents. One group of adolescents got traditional discussion-based training while another did role-play based training. The group that did role-plays experienced a significant positive change in their self-concept, which has a significant impact on their behaviors.

In our digital world, simulation training — based on role-playing real-world scenarios — is becoming increasingly popular.

Additionally, research has found that getting consistent feedback is essential to effective learning. You can use this. By making your work public, you get immediate feedback.

Getting immediate feedback has been found to be a flow trigger. It heightens performance. Especially when the feedback is real world, and there are real consequences for success and failure.

10. Focus on quantity in the beginning

"Plant a lot, harvest a few." — Seth Godin

In the book Originals: How Non-Conformists Move the World, Adam Grant explains that "originals" (i.e., people who create innovative work) are not reliable. In other words, not everything they produce is extraordinary.

For example, among the 50 greatest pieces of music ever created, six belong to Mozart, five are Beethoven's, and three Bach's. But in order to create those, Mozart wrote over 600 compositions, Beethoven 650, and Bach over 1,000.

Similarly, Picasso created thousands of pieces of art, and few are considered to be his "great works." Edison had 1,900 patents, and only a handful we would recognize. Albert Einstein published 248 scientific articles, only a few of which are what got him on the map for his theory of relativity.

Quantity is the most likely path to quality. The more you produce, the more ideas you will have — some of which will be innovative and original. And you never know which ones will click. You just keep creating.

11. Track only a few things (ignore everything else)

"If you have more than three priorities, then you don't have any." — Jim Collins in Good to Great: Why Some Companies Make the Leap...And Others Don't

If you want to improve at something, you need to quantify it. If you don't quantify it, you don't really know what's happening. As Thomas Monson explains, "When performance is measured, performance improves. When performance is measured and reported, the rate of improvement accelerates."

I can personally attest to this principle. When I started measuring a few metrics, such as each set in the gym, my income, and how much time I spend in "flow" while working, I dramatically improved in these areas. The reason is simple: tracking helped me become aware and objective about my weaknesses. Thus, I knew exactly where I should focus and could do it systematically.

12. Heighten expectation for what you can accomplish

"I think the ability of the average man could be doubled if it were demanded, if the situation demanded." — William Durant

I started working out with my current workout partner about two months ago. He's nearly 20 years older than me, and can lift substantially more weight than me.

One of the first things he told me was, "Most people never get stronger simply because they don't put themselves under the weight." As a result, our first several workouts involved me being heavily spotted while benching and squatting way more than I ever had before. The purpose was to feel the weight.

It hasn't taken long at all to increase my strength while working out with my new partner. He's raised my expectations. Yet I don't let his expectations dictate what I can do. As will be shown in the following section on mentorships, the expectations of those around you create the context for your growth and potential.

But you don't need to be bound by those expectations. For instance, just because many of my favorite writers publish twice per week, I decided to hold myself to a different standard when I started writing. In large measure, you get what you expect you will. According to Expectancy Theory, one of the core theories of motivation, motivation involves three components:

the value you place on your goal

your belief that specific behaviors will actually facilitate the outcomes you desire

your belief in your own ability to successfully execute the behaviors requisite to achieving your goals

Learn from the best. But don't be bound by their standards. Run at your own pace, even if that pace is faster than those you aspire to be like.

Mentorships

13. Surround yourself with people with higher expectations than you have

According to what psychologists call "The Pygmalion Effect," other people's expectations of you heavily influence how well you do.

When you're a child, the expectations of your parents "set the bar." Interestingly, these expectations form an invisible barrier from which it becomes very difficult to exceed.

For instance, scientific experiments have been done on fleas, wherein they've been put in a glass jar. Without the lid on the jar, the fleas can easily jump out. However, the fleas can be trained to stay in the jar by putting a lid on it. After only three days, the lid can be removed and the fleas will be constrained by an invisible mental barrier.

Not surprisingly, the "next generation" of fleas is also constrained by this new and invisible barrier. The Pygmalion effect explains why: the next generation develops the same expectations for themselves as their parents have for them.

If, however, you were to take one of those fleas out of that jar and place them in a bigger jar, surrounded by fleas jumping much higher, mirror neurons would fire and that flea would soon be able to jump higher. Mental barriers would shatter, soon to be replaced by the mental barriers of those in the new jar.

When seeking mentorships, it's important to realize that the expectations of your mentor reflect the flea's jar, and invisible barrier, as opposed to your inherent ability. There is no fixed ability. Nothing, and nobody, has an "absolute" value. Everything is contextual.

Even still, by jumping into a much bigger jar, you'll quickly grow. Actually, you may learn to jump much higher than you ever imaged with the help of a caring mentor. Thus, it is extremely important for you to surround yourself with those who have high expectations for you. It may be difficult, frustrating, and humbling to develop and grow. But if you stick to it, you'll eventually reach a new invisible cap.

14. Expect to expand and adapt

Human beings are highly adaptive. For instance, Viktor Frankl reflected on his experience as a Nazi concentration camp victim and sleeping comfortably next to nine other people on small beds. Said Frankl in Man's Search for Meaning, "Yes a person can get used to anything, just don't ask us how." Indeed, this was one of the most surprising aspects of living in a concentration camp, the rapidity at which the shock and horror became apathy and "normal."

No matter how far-reaching and discontinuous the jump from one environment to the next, a person can and will adapt, whether that means going from zero kids to three (trust me), or from completely inactive to exercising with professional bodybuilders.

Take, for example, Collin Clark, a 20-year-old who lost 64 pounds and 30 percent body fat in six months. The process was simple; he went to the gym and began to emulate the bodybuilders who were there. Eventually, one particular bodybuilder took an interest in Collin, and became his mentor. By working out daily with a bodybuilder, Collin transformed. The example of Collin Clark is particularly notable, as he has down syndrome.

When you first enter a new and larger jar, you'll feel excited and perhaps even intimidated by all the jumping room. However, like gas which spreads to fill the space it's been given, you too will adapt. Thus, you won't want to overstay your welcome. Remember, the jar is a reflection of other people's expectations.

Hence, the next point:

15. Don't get stuck with one mentor

"When the student is ready the teacher will appear. When the student is truly ready, the teacher will disappear." — Lao Tzu

High-quality friendships should last forever. High-quality mentorships, on the other hand, should not last forever.

One mentor can only take you so far; they can only give you one "jar." If you want to evolve beyond that jar, you'll need a new mentor. And this is exactly what any true mentor would want for you as well. It's not about "them." They are investing in you. It is through your best work that they can live on forever.

16. The mentor sets the expectations, but the mentee sets the tone

Although the mentor's expectations and abilities reflect the size of the jar, it is the mentee that sets the tone for the relationship and how well it will go.

I've been in mentoring relationships where I've been a good mentee and a bad mentee. In each case, it was not the mentor, but me, who determined how well the relationship went. No one cares more about your success than you do. It is up to you how far you go in life.

Darren Hardy, author of The Compound Effect, has said, "Never take advice from someone you wouldn't trade places with." Thus, you should be highly selective about the mentors you seek. If you aren't intrinsically motivated to "set the tone" with your mentor, ask yourself: Do I really want to be like this person? If the answer is no, then they are the wrong mentor.

When you have the right mentor, you'll know, because you'll feel extremely lucky to have even a few moments of their time. You'll do all you can to deepen the relationship, provide value, and learn. You'll be willing to bend over backward to help them. You'll take on greater responsibility. You'll make their life easier. You'll make them look good.

17. Give credit where credit is due

Although you are responsible for your own success, you are not the sole cause of that success. Far from it. You are not independent of all the help you've received. More accurately, you are the product of all the help you've received.

You are standing on the shoulders of giants. Acknowledge them for that. And never forget where you came from. Also, never speak poorly about your mentors or those who have helped you along your journey. This does nothing for you. I've made this mistake and destroyed important relationships with people I deeply admire — people who invested lots of time and energy into me.

As Ryan Holiday explains in his book, Ego is the Enemy, always be a student. Remain humble. Don't let ego take over, or it will lead to your inevitable demise.

Mental Models

In this final section, I will detail beliefs required for rapid growth.

18. Think astronomically

"You have nothing to lose and everything to gain." — Robin Williams

There is some brilliant new research on the concept of Awe, which has been defined as a feeling that arises when you encounter something so strikingly vast (in time, scope, complexity, ability, or power) it provokes a need to update your mental schemas.

Awe, or having a peak experience, can happen during an optimal sports performance or even a deep spiritual experience. When you become mindful, you can experience awe even during mundane moments.

Research has found that experiencing awe can expand your perception of time, alter your decision-making abilities, and enhance your well-being.

I can personally attest to these findings. I've experienced awe several times. I strive to experience it as often as possible, which for me provides a much richer and deeper perspective of life.

Awe alters your experience with time because it helps you see things more astronomically. From the perspective of light, for example, time stands still. Thus, this moment, from the perspective of light, is both an instant and an eternity. Time fades into the background of infinite possibility. Nothing becomes impossible. No distance too far.

Awe alters your ability to make decisions because you no longer fear trivial things such as other people's perceptions, failure, or even death.

Lastly, awe alters your well-being because the mind and body are one. When you improve one aspect of your life, all others organically improve as well. Thus, when you experience a deeper connection with yourself and the universe, you live differently. You see yourself differently, and that perception has the power to alter your biology. Your emotional state also matures and becomes more healthy as well.

19. Think laterally

"Lateral thinking doesn't replace hard work; it eliminates unnecessary cycles." — Shane Snow in Smartcuts: How Hackers, Innovators, and Icons Accelerate Success

Most of the United States presidents spent less time in politics than the average congressman. Moreover, the best, and most popular presidents, generally spent the least amount of time in politics. Rather than spending decades climbing the tedious ladder with glass ceilings, they simply jumped laterally from a different, non-political ladder.

Ronald Reagan was an actor. Dwight Eisenhower laterally shifted from the military. Woodrow Wilson bounced over from academia. These men spent considerably little time in politics and became fabulous presidents. They reached the top by skipping the unnecessary "dues-paying" steps. Insanely productive people think the same way. Rather than climbing up ladders the traditional ways, they think of alternative routes. They skip unnecessary steps by pivoting and shifting.

Shane Snow himself used this tactic to get published on some of the biggest media outlets in the world within six months of blogging. How did he do it? He started by pitching articles to low-level blogs with basically no bar of entry. After getting a few articles published on those, he leveraged his new position and pitched to slightly higher-level blogs.

He did this by sending editors of the slightly "better" blogs an email reading something like: Hello, I've written at these blogs which reach similar audiences as your blog. Here's an article I think would be a great fit for your audience.

Because the editors of those blogs knew about the blogs Snow had been published on, he was able to be published on theirs as well. He followed this pattern over and over until, within six months, his work was published at Fast Company, WIRED, and others.

20. Think more flexibly about "limits" on resources

One of the faultiest and most crippling mindsets people have is over-categorizing things, and then being bound by those categories. Psychologists call this having a "pre-mature cognitive commitment."

When you see things from only a singular perspective, you'll assume there is a limited supply of that thing.

Money, from most people's perspective, is a limited resource. However, research has found that after basic needs are met, what people really want is a state of mind. Yet, that state of mind doesn't have to be tightly bound within the cognitive category of money.

Consequently, from a mindful perspective, you can look at certain things, like money or even yourself, from multiple viewpoints. You don't have to get stuck with fixed and rigid definitions. In nearly any case, you come to realize that what you want is always available to you, if you'll simply alter your viewpoint. As Ellen Langer, Harvard psychologist has said, "If we examine what is behind our desires, we can usually get what we want without compromising."

The most detrimental thing we can view from a limited standpoint is ourselves. Don't let your own assumptions and categories determine what you are. You have no clue who you are or what you can become. Different angles and more flexible definitions allows for limitless possibilities.

21. Think more flexibly about "limits" on time

"It is utterly beyond our power to measure the changes of things by time." — Ernst Mach in The Science of Mechanics: A Critical and Historical Account of Its Development

Time is an abstraction, which we conceive by the change of other things. For example, the changing of the seasons, or the aging of a child.

Many people have rigid notions, for example, about how long certain things must take.

You can't finish high school until you're 18 years old.

You can't be successful until after you've paid your dues.

If you break your leg, it must take a few months to heal.

These fixed notions about time are constraining and limiting. Change can occur at different magnitudes and qualities depending on the context. For example, there is a concept called, "Spontaneous Remission," wherein an illness or disease surprisingly and immediately changes.

When I started my writing career, I was told it would take me at least three to five years to get the amount of subscribers needed to get a literary agent and subsequent book contract. I was told this by a highly credible source, actually a literary agent herself. However, that was based on her assumptions of time and resources, which resources also included my abilities and motivations.

She had no clue of my context, desires, and abilities. Thus, her assumptions about how long it would take me were absurd. Yet, she was just going off what she had seen, which caused her to be mindless about the situation. Within months of the conversation with that literary agent, I was in the position she said would take several years.

Takeaway: Let go of your beliefs about fixed limits of time. Time is a unique concept, which few of us understand. It need not be linear nor lead to entropy. Again, many scholars are seeing that these are nothing more than assumptions, or fixed mindsets about how things work.

Conclusion

Achieving your goals is very doable. It need not take as long as you may have previously assumed.

There is no fixed limit on how much you can learn and grow. There is no fixed amount of time it must take.

SEVEN

This Morning Routine will Save You 20+ Hours Per Week

Your first three hours will make or break you.

The traditional 9–5 workday is poorly structured for high productivity. Perhaps when most work was physical labor, but not in the knowledge working world we now live in.

Although this may be obvious based on people's mediocre performance, addiction to stimulants, lack of engagement, and the fact that most people hate their jobs — now there's loads of scientific evidence you can't ignore.

The Myth of the 8 Hour Workday

The most productive countries in the world do not work 8 hours per day. Actually, the most productive countries have the shortest workdays.

People in countries like Luxembourg are working approximately 30 hours per week (approximately 6 hours per day, 5 days per week) and making more money on average than people working longer work weeks.

This is the average person in those countries. But what about the super-productive?

Although Gary Vaynerchuck claims to work 20 hours per day, many "highly successful" people I know work between 3–6 hours per day.

It also depends on what you're really trying to accomplish in your life. Gary Vaynerchuck wants to own the New York Jets. He's also fine, apparently, not spending much time with his family.

And that's completely fine. He's clear on his priorities.

However, you must also be clear on yours. If you're like most people, you probably want to make a great income, doing work you love, that also provides lots of flexibility in your schedule.

If that's your goal, this post is for you.

Quality Vs. Quantity

"Wherever you are, make sure you're there." — Dan Sullivan

If you're like most people, your workday is a blend of low-velocity work mixed with continual distraction (e.g., social media and email).

Most people's "working time" is not done at peak performance levels. When most people are working, they do so in a relaxed fashion. Makes sense, they have plenty of time to get it done.

However, when you are results-oriented, rather than "being busy," you're 100 percent on when you're working and 100 percent off when you're not. Why do anything half-way? If you're going to work, you're going to work.

To get the best results in your fitness, research has found that shorter but more intensive exercise is more effective than longer drawn-out exercise.

The concept is simple: Intensive activity followed by high quality rest and recovery.

Most of the growth actually comes during the recovery process. However, the only way to truly recover is by actually pushing yourself to exhaustion during the workout.

The same concept applies to work. The best work happens in short intensive spurts. By short, I'm talking 1–3 hours. But this must be "Deep Work," with no distractions, just like an intensive workout is non-stop. Interestingly, your best work — which for most people is thinking — will actually happen while you're away from your work, "recovering."

For best results: Spend 20% of your energy on your work and 80% of your energy on recovery and self-improvement. When you're getting high quality recovery, you're growing. When you're continually honing your mental model, the quality and impact of your work continually increases. This is what psychologists call, "Deliberate Practice." It's not about doing more, but better training. It's about being strategic and results-focused, not busyness-focused.

In one study, only 16 percent of respondents reported getting creative insight while at work. Ideas generally came while the person was at home, in transportation, or during recreational activity. "The most creative ideas aren't going to come while sitting in front of your monitor," says Scott Birnbaum, a vice president of Samsung Semiconductor.

The reason for this is simple. When you're working directly on a task, your mind is tightly focused on the problem at hand (i.e., direct reflection). Conversely, when you're not working, your mind loosely wanders (i.e., indirect reflection).

While driving or doing some other form of recreation, the external stimuli in your environment (like the buildings or other landscapes around you) subconsciously prompt memories and other thoughts. Because your mind is wandering both contextually (on different subjects) and temporally between past, present, and future, your brain will make distant and distinct connections related to the problem you're trying to solve (eureka!).

Creativity, after all, is making connections between different parts of the brain. Ideation and inspiration is a process you can perfect.

Case in point: when you're working, be at work. When you're not working, stop working. By taking your mind off work and actually recovering, you'll get creative breakthroughs related to your work.

Your First Three Hours Will Make or Break You

According to psychologist Ron Friedman, the first three hours of your day are your most precious for maximized productivity.

"Typically, we have a window of about three hours where we're really, really focused. We're able to have some strong contributions in terms of planning, in terms of thinking, in terms of speaking well," Friedman told Harvard Business Review.

This makes sense on several levels. Let's start with sleep. Research confirms the brain, specifically the prefrontal cortex, is most active and readily creative immediately following sleep. Your subconscious mind has been loosely mind-wandering while you slept, making contextual and temporal connections.

So, immediately following sleep, your mind is most readily active to do thoughtful work.

So, your brain is most attuned first thing in the morning, and so are your energy levels. Consequently, the best time to do your best work is during the first three hours of your day.

I used to exercise first thing in the morning. Not anymore. I've found that exercising first thing in the morning actually sucks my energy, leaving me with less than I started.

Lately, I've been waking up at 6AM, driving to my school and walking to the library I work in. While walking from my car to the library, I drink a 250 calorie plant-based protein shake (approximately 30 grams of protein).

Donald Layman, professor emeritus of nutrition at the University of Illinois, recommends consuming at least 30 grams of protein for breakfast. Similarly, Tim Ferriss, in his book, The 4-Hour Body, also recommends 30 grams of protein 30 minutes after awaking.

Protein-rich foods keep you full longer than other foods because they take longer to leave the stomach. Also, protein keeps blood-sugar levels steady, which prevent spikes in hunger.

I get to the library and all set-up by around 6:30AM. I spend a few minutes in prayer and meditation, followed by a 5–10 minute session in my journal. The purpose of this journal session is get clarity and focus for my day.

Journaling about your dreams is one of the fastest ways into a peak state.

So I write down my big picture goals and my objectives for that particular day. I then write down anything that comes to my mind. Often, it relates to people I need to contact, or ideas related to a project I'm working on. I purposefully keep this journal session short and focused.

By 6:45, I'm set to work on whatever project I'm working on, whether that's writing a book or an article, working on a research paper for my doctoral research, creating an online course, etc.

Starting work this early may seem crazy to you, but I've been shocked by how easy it is to work for 2–5 hours straight without distractions. My mind is laser at this time of day. And I don't rely on any stimulants at all.

Between 11AM–noon, my mind is ready for a break, so that's when I do my workout. Research confirms that you workout better with food in your system. Consequently, my workouts are now a lot more productive and powerful than they were when I was exercising immediately following sleep.

After the workout, which is a great mental break, you should be fine to work a few more hours, if needed.

If your 3–5 hours before your workout were focused, you could probably be done for the day.

Protect Your Mornings

I understand that this schedule will not work for everyone. There are single-parents with kids who simply can't do something like this.

We all need to work within the constraints of our unique contexts. However, if you work best in the morning, you gotta find a way to make it happen.This may require waking up a few extra hours earlier than you're used to and taking a nap during the afternoon.

Or, it may require you to simply focus hardcore the moment you get to work.A common strategy for this is known as the "90–90–1" rule, where you spend the first 90 minutes of your workday on your #1 priority. I'm certain this isn't checking your email or social media.

Whatever your situation, protect your mornings!

I'm blown away by how many people schedule things like meetings in the mornings. Nothing could be worse for peak performance and creativity.

Schedule all of your meetings for the afternoon, after lunch.

Don't check your social media or email until after your 3 hours of deep work. Your morning time should be spent on output, not input.

If you don't protect your mornings, a million different things will take up your time. Other people will only respect you as much as you respect yourself.

Protecting your mornings means you are literally unreachable during certain hours. Only in case of a serious emergency can you be summoned from your focus-cave.

Mind-Body Connection

What you do outside work is just as significant for your work-productivity as what you do while you're working.

A March 2016 study in the online issue of Neurology found that regular exercise can slow brain aging by as much as 10 years. Loads of other research has found that people who regularly exercise are more productive at work. Your brain is, after all, part of your body. If your body is healthier, it makes sense that your brain would operate better.

If you want to operate at your highest level, you need to take a holistic approach to life. You are a system. When you change a part of any system, you simultaneously change the whole. Improve one area of your life, all other areas improve in a virtuous cycle. This is the butterfly effect in action and the basis of the book, The Power of Habit, which shows that by integrating one "keystone habit," like exercise or reading, that the positivity of that one habits ripples into all other areas of your life, eventually transforming your whole life.

Consequently, the types of foods you eat, and when you eat them, determine your ability to focus at work. Your ability to sleep well (by the way, it's easy to sleep well when you get up early and work hard) is also essential to peak-performance. Rather than managing your time, then, you should really be focused on managing your energy. Your work schedule should be scheduled around when you work best, not around social norms and expectations.

Don't Forget to Psychologically Detach and Play

Research in several fields has found that recovery from work is a necessity for staying energetic, engaged, and healthy when facing job demands.

"Recovery" is the process of reducing or eliminating physical and psychological strain/stress caused by work.

One particular recovery strategy that is getting lots of attention in recent research is called "psychological detachment from work." True psychological detachment occurs when you completely refrain from work-related activities and thoughts during non-work time.

Proper detachment/recovery from work is essential for physical and psychological health, in addition to engaged and productive work. Yet, few people do it. Most people are always "available" to their email and work. Millennials are the worst, often wearing the openness to work "whenever" as a badge of honor. It's not a badge of honor.

Research has found that people who psychologically detach from work experience:

Less work-related fatigue and procrastination

Far greater engagement at work, which is defined as vigor, dedication, and absorption (i.e., "flow")

Greater work-life balance, which directly relates to quality of life

Greater marital satisfaction

Greater mental health

When you're at work, be fully absorbed. When it's time to call it a day, completely detach yourself from work and become absorbed in the other areas of your life.

If you don't detach, you'll never fully be present or engaged at work or at home. You'll be under constant strain, even if minimally. Your sleep will suffer. Your relationships will be shallow. Your life will not be happy.

Not only that, but lots of science has found play to be extremely important for productivity and creativity. Just like your body needs a reset, which you can get through fasting, you also need to reset from work in order to do your best work. Thus, you need to step away from work and dive into other beautiful areas of your life. For me, that's goofing off with my kids.

Stuart Brown, founder of the National Institute for Play, has studied the "Play Histories" of over six thousand people and concludes playing can radically improve everything — from personal well-being to relationships to learning to an organization's potential to innovate. As Greg McKeown explains, "Very successful people see play as essential for creativity."

In his TED talk, Brown said, "Play leads to brain plasticity, adaptability, and creativity... Nothing fires up the brain like play." There is a burgeoning body of literature highlighting the extensive cognitive and social benefits of play, including:

Cognitive

Enhanced memory and focus

Improved language learning skills

Creative problem solving

Improved mathematics skills

Increased ability to self-regulate, an essential component of motivation and goal achievement

Social

Cooperation

Team work

Conflict resolution

Leadership skill development

Control of impulses and aggressive behavior

Having a balanced-life is key to peak performance. In the Tao Te Ching, it explains that being too much yin or too much yang leads to extremes and being wasteful with your resources (like time). The goal is to be in the center, balanced.

Listen to Brain Music or Songs on Repeat

In her book, On Repeat: How Music Plays the Mind, psychologist Elizabeth Hellmuth Margulis explains why listening to music on repeat improves focus. When you're listening to a song on repeat, you tend to dissolve into the song, which blocks out mind wandering (let your mind wander while you're away from work!).

Wordpress founder, Matt Mullenweg, listens to one single song on repeat to get into flow. So do authors Ryan Holiday and Tim Ferriss, and many others.

Give it a try.

You can use this website to listen to YouTube video's on repeat.

I generally listen to classical music or electronic music (like video game type music). Here's a few that have worked for me:

One Moment by Michael Nyman

Make Love by Daft Punk

Tearin' it up by Gramatik

Terra's theme from Final Fantasy 3

Duel of Fates from Star Wars

Stop crying your heart out by Oasis

Give up by Eligah Bossenbroek (so beautiful)

Heart by Stars

This cover of Ellie Goulding

Fragile by Daft Punk

Son of Flynn by Daft Punk

Cool by Alesso

Sun Through the Clouds by Matthew Morgan

Testing by CKY

Borderline by Madonna

Every You and Every Me by Placebo

Main Titles composed by Alan Menken for The Little Mermaid

Halcyon On and On by Orbital

There Goes the Fear by Doves

Never Follow Suit by The Radio Dept.

These days, I mostly use Focus@Will (I have no affiliation).

EIGHT

10 HABITS OF ONLY 1% PEOPLE

Success is something that we all want. We've read about it, heard about it, fantasized about it, and even watched movies about it. But how many of us are actually able to achieve success?

Successful people have many things in common. They all know their strengths, they never rest on their laurels and they are always willing to learn more. Are you familiar with the term "best practices"?

It describes a situation when something is done in an ideal way. It means the best possible solution was found to a problem. And all can be done through a well-designed system.

What does that mean?

A system is responsible for the results, and you are responsible for the system!

A system is a structure that you make, which helps you get a certain approach towards problems!

Let me make it simple.

The system is your mindset. You design your mindset through habits. This process trains your subconscious mind and when you need to make a quick decision — your subconscious mind reacts as it has been trained!

Some people make the systems that help them to grow and some people make such systems that keep them holding back.

Hence, we all need to make a better system that can help us to succeed. Following are some habits that I studied, implemented, and got incredible results.

I want to share with you the 10 habits of only 1% of people (Successful people).

1. Scheduling

One of the most common things we hear from successful people is that they schedule their time.

They understand that it takes time and effort to achieve goals. Time management isn't about squeezing every minute of the day; it's about making the most of your minutes.

How important is time scheduling, really? It can be the difference between a life where you get everything done and one where you don't.

2. Planning

Most of us think we're capable of achieving success without planning, but that's not true.

Successful people know planning is the key to greatness. They plan their days, weeks, years, and every other aspect of their lives. Planning is the most important step to success.

You can make decisions but you don't know what will happen. It doesn't mean things happen from high power or none of us has any control. The point is, your decisions are going to affect the life of each and every person who is connected to you. It's not written, but it's being written!

You need a plan, a backup plan, and a second backup plan. Backup is the only way, they don't change the destination.

For example, If you want to go from New York to San Fransisco. Your first plan is to take a flight (just to save time). For some reason, the flight got canceled. You should've got an option for a train. Or you can take a bus! what worse could happen. Just start walking on a road and take lifts from trucks... I know it's not a good example but you get the point, right?

The first step to planning your life is to create a vision statement. A vision statement is a detailed description of what you want to achieve in your life, including your professional and personal goals.

3. Waking Up Early

Many successful people wake up early to exercise, meditate or do something that they love.

The most successful CEOs and entrepreneurs like Richard Branson, Elon Musk, Mark Cuban, Oprah Winfrey, and many others wake up early.

Waking up early, at least an hour before other people in your household, is the secret weapon of successful people.

It allows you to schedule your day to be more productive and accomplish a lot more with your time. It's one of the best ways to get ahead.

4. Meditating

Meditation is a practice that allows you to concentrate on different types of thoughts. It's about quieting your mind and focusing on the present.

When you meditate, you train your attention on one thing for a set amount of time.

It doesn't have to be an hour-long session with incense burning and candles lit. It can be as simple as sitting quietly for 10 minutes.

Meditation can reduce stress, anxiety, and depression, and it improves focus, concentration, memory, and creativity.

5. Exercise Daily

Exercise is an important part of being healthy and successful.

There are countless studies that show the benefits of exercise and there are numerous benefits to a healthy lifestyle.

The first step is finding out what works for you. You don't want to spend hours in the gym every day if you really don't enjoy it, but you also don't want to skip it every day because you think it's a waste of time.

You're going to have to experiment with different activities and find something that makes you happy.

If you do this once, you'll be able to make exercise a daily habit.

6. Staying Disconnected From Phone

It doesn't mean that you just throw away your phone. Because at present time. we work on our phones. We cannot switch off or turn off the data.

The best way I found is to turn off the notification of all social media apps and not to put them on the home screen.

A phone is just a tool, it's not good or bad. Our use of phones can be quantified.

Now it's a challenge for all of us, how much we are capable, serious, and mentally strong to achieve our goals!

7. Reading

Successful people are readers. They read to learn new things, to gain a new perspective, and to be inspired and motivated.

But why do they read?

The one thing I believe is that successful people read a lot because most of us our information is in text form. They also listen to audiobooks and watch documentaries.

But reading has an advantage over listening and watching. It improves your memory, imagination, and creativity. It lets you imagine without any boundaries.

8. Listen To New Ideas

Successful people are hungry for new ideas. They always want to be learning. That's how they stay ahead of the pack and how they find new opportunities.

When you get your mind into learning mode, you open yourself up to new ideas and possibilities, and that's when you can find the next big thing.

9. Saving To Invest

I've read a lot of personal finance books, and one thing I've noticed is that almost all of them encourage people to invest early and often.

The reason they say that is because the earlier you start investing, the sooner you'll reach the point when your investments will make more money than you spend each month.

At this point, you can spend that extra income on whatever you like because it's essentially free money.

10. Work With Inner Motivation

Inner motivation is the most important thing that makes a person successful. This is something that people usually don't know about, but it's true.

There are people who are highly motivated by external factors like money, fame, or awards. But deep inside them, they have no motivation to work on their goals and dreams.

On the other hand, there are people who are motivated to work for their own benefit and success. They do not need any motivation from outside sources to make them work.

These people can get up in the morning and write down their goals.

NINE

5 Reasons To Rise At 5 AM By Robin Sharma

It's no secret that early birds get the worm.

Photo by Andreas Fickl

Waking up early has its own perks, and those who rise with the sun are better off than their night owls.

Productivity is a huge part of my life, and I have found that rising at 5 AM every day really helps me to prioritize it.

There are tons of different tips and tricks out there on how to become an early riser, but here are the top five reasons that I heard from Robin Sharma and it helped me to be better at productivity.

1. It's Deeply Peaceful

It's a strange thing: When it's dark and quiet outside, I feel a deep sense of peace. I'm not alone.

Many people share this sentiment, and I've noticed this trend as I've grown older. The world is crazy right now. Daily news reports are filled with stories of violence and fear, and technology has made our lives faster and more complicated at the same time.

These days, we struggle to find time to just sit still and be. This happens because we don't have time for ourselves.

It's a good habit to rise early, sit with yourself for half an hour and start your day taking some time to reboot your brain.

2. You'll Grow In Willpower

There are several benefits of rising early. In fact, it can help you with your willpower. Early risers have been shown to be more proactive, productive, and successful than late risers.

The average person in the West wakes up at 7:00 AM. They spend about 70–90 minutes brushing their teeth, taking a shower, and eating breakfast. Then head to work.

If you get up at 5:00 AM, you will have 2 hours extra each day, 14 hours a week, and 60 hours a month.

During those hours, you can do anything that is totally related to you. For example:

You can work on your side hustle.

You can read a book.

Workout & Yoga.

Meditation for straight 30 minutes.

There are lots of things you can do. This is how you can make your life better.

3. You Can Work Out To Get Fitter

Everybody knows that the most time for exercise is in the morning. It's much easier to go jogging or to a gym in the early morning, than at night or in the afternoon.

But no one does it because we are sleepy and tired then.

If you are into physical fitness, then you know how it feels to get up early in the morning for a workout session.

However, as time goes by, working out in the morning is becoming a thing of the past. Nowadays, more and more people are choosing to work out at night.

I have gathered some benefits of working out in the morning:

Fewer distractions.

More overall energy.

Better focus.

Better mood.

Improved sleep.

4. It's A Beautiful Time To Read Wisdom

If you rise early, the morning sun feels a bit warmer, the air smells a bit fresher than it does later in the day.

And if you get up before the crack of dawn, you can actually read a book with that beautiful light coming through your window.

The world is full of distractions, and it's hard to find time to read but this is your chance. Put on some coffee, wake up early, and start reading.

5. You'll 5x You Productivity

"The secret of your future is hidden in your daily routine." -Mike Murdoch

What if I told you that you could get 5 times more done than the average person? It's not a trick question. It's not clickbait. It's true.

You can. If you were to wake up 2 hours before everyone else and work for those 2 hours, in the morning, before anyone else is around and interruptions are at a minimum you could easily get 5 times as much done as if you waited until later in the day and worked during regular business hours

TEN

HOW I IMPROVED MY MEMORY AND CONCENTRATION

Everyone wants to improve their mind and concentration. We want to be able to focus on the task at hand, without becoming distracted by everything else going on around us.

The good news is that it's possible. It's important to understand how your brain works to improve your focus. Understanding how it works will allow you to tap into your full potential.

Your brain has three main processing functions: sensory, short-term memory, and long-term memory.

For example, when you are watching a movie, your brain processes the sights and sounds you see and hear through sensory processing.

Short-term Memory

Short-term memory is the ability to hold small amounts of information in mind for a brief period. It's responsible for helping us remember what we had for breakfast this morning, but not much else.

Long-term Memory

Long-term memory is the system in your brain that handles longer-lasting information.

This can include facts and events that you have experienced, learned, or otherwise internalized. Long-term memory is where both implicit and explicit knowledge resides.

You're using long-term memory when you recall your childhood home, remember how to ride a bike or play an instrument or do math in your head.

You're also using long-term memory when you remember what it feels like to be rejected, insulted, or ignored. These memories are especially powerful because they are associated with emotions.

So we have understood the brain functions that are involved in learning. Now I am going to share 5 tips on training the mind for better learning and concentration.

Read Everyday

"You may not realize it, but you're a reader," said Francis Bacon, one of the founding fathers of the scientific method.

You read something every time you look at your phone or computer, even if it's just a few words from an app like Twitter or Google.

These words are building up and improving your mind, even if you don't realize it.

Reading books is a completely different experience. It takes effort to get through them, but the effort pays off.

You'll start noticing subtle patterns in language and you'll pick up on things that will aid you in your personality.

Exercise Regularly

No doubt exercising regularly has a positive impact on your body, but it also does a lot for your mind. Just like writing, exercise helps you learn and grow as a person.

"If you want to be creative, if you want to be innovative, if you want to be a leader, you have to do uncomfortable things. You have to go out of your comfort zone." — Steve Jobs

There is lots of scientific evidence that exercise is good for your mind. It can help to reduce stress and anxiety, improve your mood, and even increase your level of focus and attention.

Write Down Ideas

I love ideas. I collect them, I write them down, and I even talk to my friends about them. Ideas are the source of all change.

Without ideas, we would be stagnant and boring.

I have been thinking about writing down my ideas for a long time, but it used to feel like a terrible idea.

I feared that if I put my ideas out there, someone would steal them and make a bunch of money off of me without giving me anything in return.

This line of thinking is very common among people who have never had their ideas stolen before.

Don't worry, not everyone dares to accomplish those ideas, execution demands lots of effort and courage.

The mind needs inspiration and motivation to perform at the highest level. Every day, take time to write down ideas that will help you stay energized and focused on your goals.

Get Out Of The Comfort Zone

Learning new things is one of the best ways to develop your mind.

However, most people don't want to expand their knowledge because they are too comfortable with what they already know.

However, it's important to get out of your comfort zone if you want to improve your mind.

Facing a new challenge every day will help you become more efficient in solving problems and thinking outside the box.

When you start learning something new, you will also be more enthusiastic about doing other things that were once hard for you. It's one of the easiest ways to change your life.

Create New Healthy Habits

The human mind is like a muscle. The more you work it and train it, the stronger it gets. The same is true for your mind.

If you want to increase your ability to focus, pay attention, and remain calm in stressful situations then you need to create new habits that train your mind and force it to adapt to these new behaviors.

If you want to develop new healthy habits that can improve your life, and ultimately the lives of those around you, focus on one habit at a time.

Give yourself 4 weeks to work on it and you will start feeling changes in yourself.

ELEVEN

HOW I LEARNT TO SPEAK FLUENT ENGLISH IN NO TIME?

Which you can do too to learn any language

Me, a 25 year old, from a small village in India, where globalization is the future and English speaking ability is measure for intelligence, there was no other way for me than to improve and adapt.

Since you are here, you are keen to improvise your language abilities, hence I will not waste more time on introduction but will get to the points straight away.

What you can do to improve your english?

1. Read books aloud—

Since you are here, I am assuming you know how to read, write and speak basic English, so you will wonder why I am giving this age old ancient advice to you. Answer is clear, what works works, what doesn't doesn't.

When I was newly out of school and a freshman in College, I was comparatively good in writing in English, but speaking, oh heck no! ? I was in that category of people who respond to "How are you?" as "I am fine", because I did not know anything better, I was lacking the skills to explain my emotions, sometimes I knew what to say but I didn't have knowledge of how to say. That's when books came to my rescue. I am big fan of Self help books, so I used to binge read them on my way to college in train.

That's when I noticed a pattern, often I knew what a word meant, and how to pronounce it, but when the time used to come to say it out loud, my mouth somehow used to forget how to say it. God that embarrassment! ?

To conquer this, I started reading out loud, somehow listening to your own voice works wonders, the mistakes you make become loud and clear, for you to understand and correct. And don't worry! you do not have to read aloud in public, do it in the safe space called home! And that's it you are on to your first step.

P. S.— Read the books you like, there are so many benefits, I can't even explain ??

2. Netflix is your friend—

No-No! I am not telling you to go buy Netflix subscription right away. I am telling you to start watching English content, be it series, movies or even documentaries. If you want a starting point Brooklyn nine nine, and Big Bang Theory are my favorites in comedy genre.

Just expose yourself to new experiences, even watching content in other languages and viewing English subtitles along with, have proven benefits, as it improves your reading speed. Another reason to tune in to your favorite k-drama. wink* wink*. Try it for a few days, You can watch prime time news for starters, or even listen to some pop songs ???

3. Gamified Learning—

There are many games on playstore, which claim to help in your learning journey, the one I have used and loved is Elevate. It has simple sets of games which focus on improving your reading, writing, speaking and math skills, a good app all over. It is very useful for students as well as working professionals where expressing your ideas clearly becomes essential task. You will feel a surge of joy when you see yourself winning in these games. Also you do not have to purchase the premium version, basic version is more than enough for the daily use. A great start to success! ?

4. Communicate, Communicate, Communicate—

Yeah, I know you feel embarrassed when that grammatical mistake happens all of sudden, me too friend, me too!! I feel your feelings but we all learn from our mistakes. The one sure shot way I have experienced is to converse with your close friends in English, it does not have to be a well-rehearsed formal communication, start with simple informal bite-size conversations, like "how was your day", "what are you planning to do on this weekend" Like this. These are some of the open ended questions, for which the other person can respond according to his wishes, and you will have more opportunity to ask follow-up questions and keep the conversation running.

The key here is to converse with your trusted people, that way they can help you correct your grammar and you will not feel that intense shame, because deep down you'll know that you are doing this for your own growth. By doing this experiment with people you know and trust, be it your spouse, best friend or gym mate, the added advantage is that those people know you personally, they know your strengths and weaknesses, so they can explain your blunders lovingly and kindly. ❣?

5. Consistency is key—

Keep up the hard-work my friend, small setbacks are okay but dont get discouraged and leave your learning all of a sudden, always remember why you are working on this, you are doing this for your own success, your own growth. Some bonus points which could not make it to the list are :

1. There many informative channels out there on YouTube, which focus on grammar, so checkout those— the one I watch : linguamarina ??

2. Always google synonyms, pronunciation and meanings of difficult words.— I use this trick while writing formal emails, it leaves a good impact on receiver.

3. Try Gratitude Journal— or any type of journaling in usual, it helps to clear your mind, and your processing ability to express complicated thoughts will increase. Improved mental health is added bonus. ?

If you have read this far and liked my content, do follow my account, I will bring new content every week. A cheers to our friendship pal, watch out this space for more interesting content and stories.

TWELVE

How I manage my anxiety by using these simple apps?

If you are someone like me who suffers from anxiety and finds it exhausting to cope up with daily tasks,

Below list is for you my friend ♥

Without a further ado, here's number one:

1. Wysa — an AI chatbot:

Many a times we feel a surge of emotions, but we do not feel safe enough to share those feelings with our friends and family, at that time this app will come in handy. I have been personally using this for 3+ years and it has helped me in many situations where I was feeling sad.

The prevailing pandemic was one such situation, where everything was feeling gloomy, lifeless and everyone has suffered loneliness. ?

This apps AI is very powerful and responds to your sentences accurately almost 95% of the time. It also gives a different outlook to looking at the situation. It has been created with mental health professionals, comprising a certain set of data in it, through which you can analyse your conversations for a fresh perspective.

The conversations are completely anonymous and there's also a helpline to call in the worst case scenario kind of situation.

Overall you get a Imaginary friend close to you every second of the day. ??

2. Calm — Meditation and Sleep stories :

A calm mind is indicator of success, where a noisy mind is of chaos. If your mind is continuously cluttered with thoughts it becomes difficult to categorise which are helpful and which are downright intrusive. At such times meditation come in handy to maintain a balanced state of mind. For my fellow friends who are going through depression, please try meditation once, any platform like this can be useful. ?

There are many videos available on YouTube as well. I have suggested this app because it has a facility of daily meditation audios, where you can gain wisdom about a different topic each day, which removes the boringness of repeating same procedure everyday.

It also has other features like soundscapes, sleep stories and acoustic music at your fingertips. Do try meditation once and let me know your experience ?

3. Tusk — To do list :

Sometimes it becomes difficult to keep track of even simple tasks and you get buried under a pile of unfinished tasks, waiting for you to act on them. This becomes quite a threatening and stressful situation for me, so I use a simple and easy to use app tusk. This does not have any over the top unnecessary features, absolutely free and easy to use. ☑

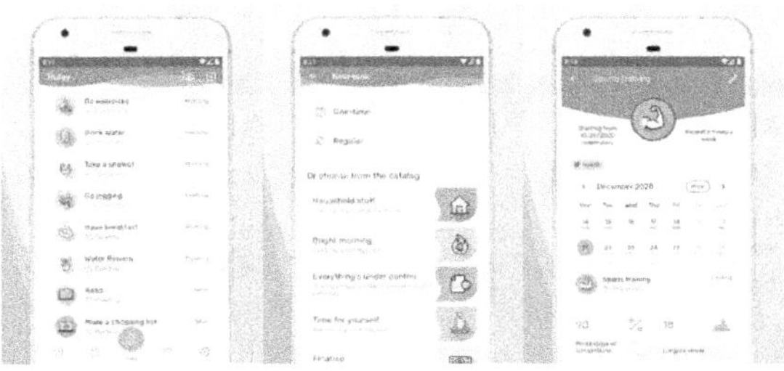

It follows the definition of to-do list app perfectly. For a simpler person like me I like my apps to obey single responsibility principle. The gist of it is that a when we try to be all at once, we dont even be good at one. This is a continuous problem with many apps of today, whereas at tusk you get a simple and easy to manage task list with some serene color theme. Want to manage your anxiety, manage your task list ?

4. Fortune City — Expense Tracker App :

So you were feeling down one fine day, saw an advertisement, went on shopping and spent a big chunk of your hard earned money in a one fine day and now you are regretting. If you want to avoid this situation use a expense tracker app. I personally follow the envelope approach to budgeting. Where we allocate a certain amount of money to each area of life, which we call as fund. For example you always prefer eating out and want to keep your spendings in check, you would select an amount as per your preferences, let's say you spend 100 dollars each month to eating out at KFC, then you will allocate 100 dollars in Food Fund. ?

The mandatory execution here is to add an entry in the expense tracker app each time you spend some money in this area. Once you reach this limit, you will stop eating out until next month. This gives you the power to manage your spendings without feeling bad about it.

Now to why I have recommended this app, because it is gamification of the cumbersome task of money management and turns it into a fun way of enjoyment.

You will feel much more calm and motivated when you will see a city flourishing because of your good habit of expense tracking. A good money saving trick is to use the free version itself. More power to you ?

5. Elevate— Language improvisation :

When you feel down certainly everyday, it becomes difficult to learn new things and master new skills. In such days, all we feel is lethargy and tiredness, somehow the drive to perform activities vanishes, in those days this app comes in handy. It has sinple sets of games which focus on improving your reading, writing, speaking and math skills, a good app all over. ?

It is useful for students as well as working professionals where expressing your ideas clearly becomes essential task. You will feel a surge of joy when you see yourself winning in these games. Also you do not have to purchase the premium version, basic version is more than enough for the daily use. A great start to success! ?

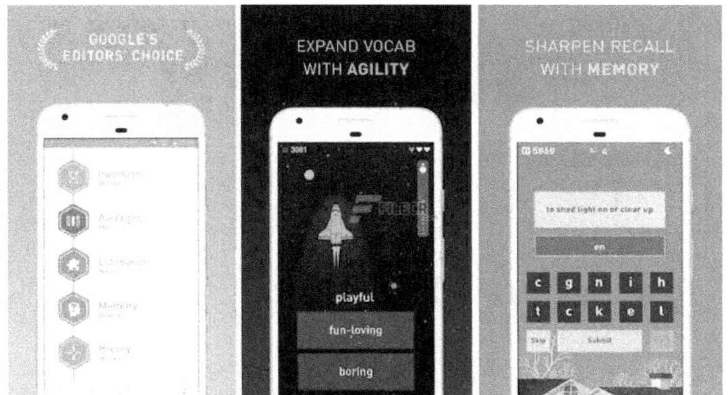
GOOGLE'S
EDITORS' CHOICE
EXPAND VOCAB
WITH AGILITY
SHARPEN RECALL
WITH MEMORY
playful
fun-loving
boring
to shed light on or clear up
en
c g n i h
t c k e l
Skip Submit

THIRTEEN

THE BOOK THAT MADE MY DAILY ACTIONS BETTER

How I do things in every aspect of my life has tremendously improved when I applied tips from this book

Do you ever set a goal but never end up accomplishing it? Do you say you're going to add something to your routine and only end up three steps backward from where you started after a few days or weeks? Do you feel like there is a gap between the person you are and the person you want to be? Have you been searching for effective ways to make your new habits automatic and ways to break free from bad habits? The book Atomic Habits by James Clear provides practical tips and answers to these deep questions. The author explains the concepts in the book through evidence from research, neuroscience, and psychology along with examples of business, education, sports, history, and simple math.

In this blog, I will be summarizing the book where I'll highlight five pearls of wisdom from this book; the power of 1% change each day in the long term, why systems are more powerful than goals, the three layers of behavior change, the steps to build better habits, and the four laws of behavior change.

1. The Power of 1% Change in the Long term

James defined habits as the compound interest of self-improvement. Compounding can both work for or against your desired habits over time. For example, as the figure below illustrates, getting 1% better each day at something will produce almost (1.01^365) 37 times better results after one year. But if I get 1% worse every day, I will go down to (0.99^365) nearly zero. The effects of a habit get magnified the more we do it.

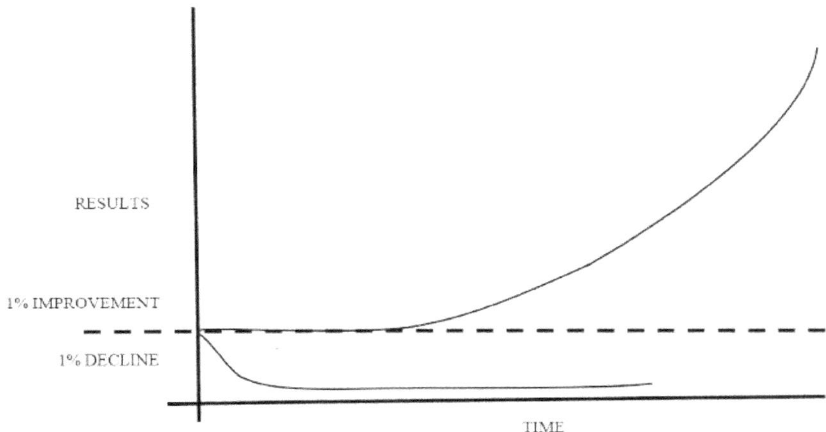

The power of 1% change each day in the long term

As humans, we often seek instant gratification and tend not to focus on small changes because it takes a long time to see the accumulated results. For example, you do not notice a difference in your body after exercising one day. However, over time the exercises you have been doing will compound to a significant and noticeable result in your body.

The author writes in the book some amazing words along the lines of this quote:

A slight change in your daily habits can guide your life to a very different destination. Making a choice that is 1% better or worse seems insignificant in the moment, but over the span of moments those choices make up a lifetime and determine the difference between who you are and who you could be. Success is the product of daily habits — not once-in-a-lifetime transformations. It does not matter how successful or unsuccessful you are right now. What matters is whether your habits are putting you on the path towards your desired success. You should be far more concerned with your current trajectory that with your current results.

I know it is not easy to maintain a good habit when you do not immediately get the rewards of your actions. We expect progress to be linear and get frustrated during the initial stages of putting in hard work. However, as the figure below shows, the most compelling outcomes are realized when we cross a critical threshold that allows us to get to breakthrough moments.

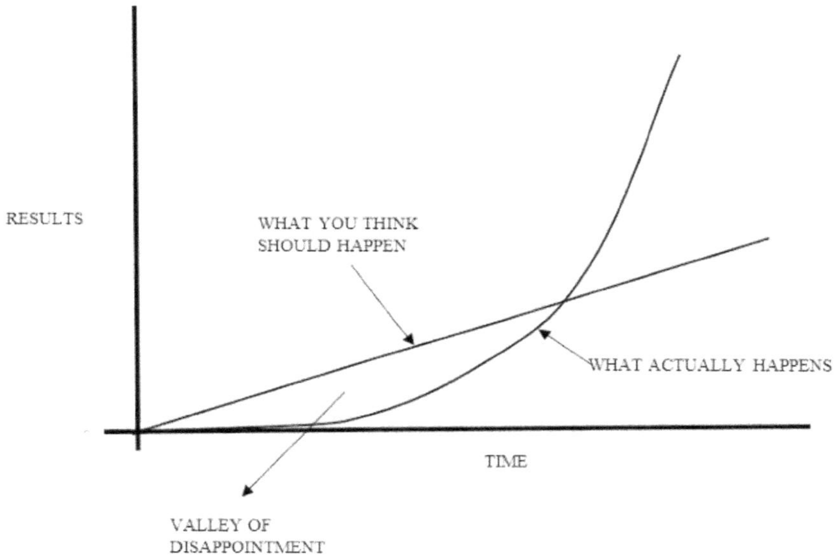

How progress looks like

2. Why Systems are More Powerful than Goals

For many years my approach to anything I wanted to achieve in life was more concentrated on setting goals until recently when I decided to focus on the systems I follow. James distinguishes the two concepts in the book; the first is about the results you want to achieve, while the latter is about the processes that lead to those results. Goals are not useless — the author writes, they are great for providing direction. But systems are best for making progress. To make this clear, James identifies four problems with goals.

(i) Winners and losers have the same goals

The problem with goals is that they suffer what the author calls "survivorship bias" — the assumption that goal setting leads to success while ignoring all of the people who had the same aim but did not succeed. Therefore, it cannot be the goal that differentiates you from every other candidate who wants the job, every other student who wants to achieve that same grade or every other Olympian who wants to win the gold medal or every other politician who wants to win the hearts of the voters.

(ii) Achieving a goal is only a momentary change

Imagine someone who has a habit of throwing stuff all over their office every day only to clean and organize when the mess gets unavoidable. They might be able to tidy up the space some days. But if they continue the habits and systems that led them to the dirty office in the first place, they will be left with the same mess. In the same way, achieving a goal changes our life only for the moment with temporary results. Instead, what we need to change is the system that initially causes those results if we want to enjoy the long-lasting benefits of our work.

(iii) Goals restrict your happiness

The author argues that behind any goal, most people assume that they will be happy once they achieve it which puts happiness on mute until later. Since we all have endless things that we want to do and get throughout our lives, such a thought process ties our happiness to a goal that might take a lifetime to achieve.

(iv) Goals are at odds with long-term progress

It is always good to look beyond your goals and ask yourself this powerful question from the book; "If I focus all my hard work on this particular goal, what will push me forward after I achieve it?". Because, for example, you might exercise for months, but if you stop as soon as you hit your desired fitness goal, you will end up reversing the progress already made.

Amazing quote from the book;

The purpose of setting goals is to win the game. The purpose of building systems is to continue playing the game. If you want results, then forget about setting goals. Focus on your system instead.

3. The Three Layers of Behavior Change

The three layers of behavior change are outcomes, process, and identity, as depicted in the figure below.

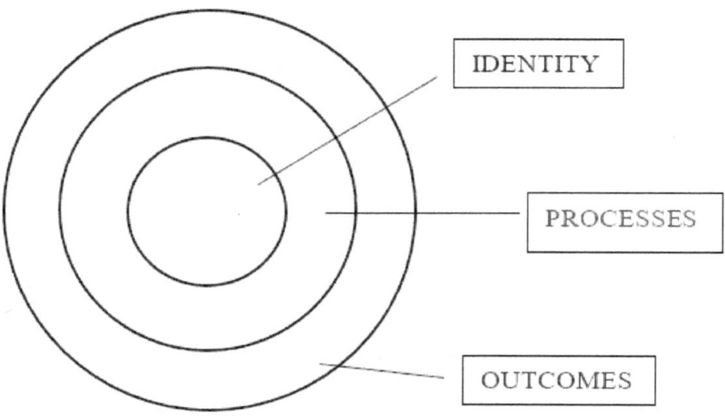

The 3 layers of behavior change

The first layer is concerned with changing our results. The second layer is about changing the process. It is related to our habits and systems. The third deepest is identity change which involves our beliefs.

Although all levels come in handy in different ways, we should focus on whom we want to become (the identity-based approach) to build a sustainable habit. Because our identity emerges out of what we repeatedly do and believe. James writes in the book; the ultimate form of intrinsic motivation is when a habit becomes part of your identity. To say I am a person who wants to read or write is different from saying I am a reader and a writer. Similarly, saying I am a person who wants to eat healthily and exercise is different from saying I am a healthy person.

True behavior change is identity change. You might start a habit because of motivation, but the only reason you will stick with one is that it becomes part of your identity. Anyone can convince themselves to visit the gym or eat healthy once or twice, but if you do not shift the belief behind the behavior, then it is hard to stick with long-term changes. Improvements are only temporary until they become part of who we are.

James Clear, Atomic Habits

4. The Steps to Build Better Habits

Now that you know that a 1% change in each day pays dividends in the long term, the reasons why you should focus more on setting systems once you know your goals and that your identity forms from what you repeatedly do, you might be asking yourself; how do I build habits?

Building a habit of any kind takes time and goes through a process before it becomes a ritual we effortlessly do. The author of this book divides the process of building habits into the following four-step patterns.

Cue: what triggers our brains to initiate an action. It is a want or a need for a reward that triggers our brain to act at this stage. This step teaches us to design our environment around the cues of what we want to achieve. Also, do the opposite for the bad habits you want to break.

Craving: the motivational force to act. This is the change you desire to see. The reason that keeps you going.

Response: the thought, action, or habit we perform. This step teaches us to assess our ability to work towards what we desire and how we need to act accordingly.

Reward: the end goal of our actions. For example, we eat food for the hunger it relieves us from and the feeling it leaves us with after eating it and not just for the sake of eating. Similarly, humans chase rewards because they give us a sense of satisfaction, fulfillment, and accomplishment.

5. The Four Laws of Behavior Change

James writes in the book the following four laws of behavior change which I found applicable. To build a good habit;

Make it obvious.

Make it attractive.

Make it easy.

Make it satisfying.

The author explains these laws through the steps of building habits, research findings, and fascinating concepts — such as an implementation intention, habit stacking, dopamine spikes, temptation bundling, finding your tribe, priming your environment, mastering decisive moments, commitment devices, a habit tracker, reinforcement techniques, habit contracts, and an accountability partner.

Finally, the inverse of the above laws become the laws of bad behavior change. So, to break free from a bad habit;

Make it invisible.

Make it unattractive.

Make it difficult.

Make it unsatisfying.

This book has changed my approach to habits in every aspect of my life; I hope you take something good away from this summary.

FOURTEEN

10 Habits To Become More Productive In Life

Productivity is the reason for living a happy life

Productivity is something which I found, personally, exciting. I can no longer work for even 5 mins if I am not in the chain or the behavior of productiveness. So productivity and being productive are essential for me. I prioritize and manage things, schedule my goals, and make a proper timetable every day, just to calm my mind and find satisfaction. That is the reason why being productive every day is so much important for me because it helps me to achieve most of the goals in my life easier.

So, if you are also like me or want a better life by being productive every single day, you have to follow some of the best practices to make your life more productive.

Here are some best practices that I follow in my daily life to become more productive (You can follow the same):

Wake up Early and Exercise

I wake up at 5:30 A.M every single day, consistently, and the first thing that I do, after making up my bed, is to exercise for at least 30–40 minutes. This makes me happier and more satisfied with my results and achievements.

Waking up early means getting most of the work done as soon as you start your day. This sets a routine for you.

Doing a high-intensity workout early in the morning can kill laziness and make you feel productive.

Divide your Work into 3 parts

Dividing your daily work and important tasks into 2 or more parts helps you tackle them very easily and effectively. I divide all my important and critical tasks into 3 categories — difficult, medium, and easy.

The difficult types of work used to be done in the morning itself, because I found myself most energetic in the morning. The medium type of work is to be done in the evenings when I find myself a bit lazy. And the easiest types of work must be tackled during the night or during the late evening.

Make a Proper timetable

Make a proper Timetable or a To-Do-List to tackle your crucial and most important tasks every single day. It is the most effective practice that I follow every single day and this really helps in tackling various tasks every day.

A proper timetable or To-Do is a good way to keep a track of your daily routine.

Tick off the work you've completed and you'll feel you've been productive.

Follow People Who Motivates you to do more

Stop wasting time on social media following people who don't motivate you to get back to work.

There are various types of people, celebrity stars, Influencers, creators, etc who are giving such friendly, positive and motivating content every single day. Follow them. Know their strengths and get inspiration from them.

Change your Workspace

Workspace is a very important place that you must take care of if you want to be more productive in life. Update or manage your workspace if you find something irrelevant or not use things in your table. Make your workspace clean and full of useful and productive things. Get rid and eliminate of things that you find useless.

Your workspace is where you spend most of your time, so make sure it makes you feel motivated to work.

In case you are bored of your workspace, shift it to a new room, preferably that has windows for fresh air.

Delegate

It is one of the most effective techniques for many Entrepreneurs and many successful people. The Art of delegation is very important in life to become more productive.

If there are some tasks which you find to be less important, but more Urgent then you must delegate them to someone else. Delegating tasks helps you to focus on other important things in life and helps you to become more productive.

You can also delegate those tasks which you're not enjoying and which can ultimately make you less productive.

Save Energy

Save your energy as much as you can. Do not get angry, frustrated, or stressed out. These all will drain your energy and will make you lazy and off from work.

Eat nutritious and healthy foods to get some more energy so that you can feel refreshed and can tackle your work very easily.

Get a Shower whenever you feel sleepy.

Avoid Procrastination.

Stop watching useless things on the internet.

More Energy = More Work Done = More Productivity = More Happier you become.

Divide your Goals

Divide your goals into yearly, monthly, weekly, and daily goals to make them seem achievable.

Plan real-time actions to achieve those goals within the deadline you've set for them.

Manage Stress

When you are forcing yourself to multi-task, stress is definitely going to cover you. Managing stress is the first thing you can do to become more productive.

Whenever you feel stressed from work, go and do something which you really enjoy besides work. Like you can walk around nature (with no phone and technological gadgets), do positive self-talk, talk with your friends, write about your problems, take a rest, etc.

Take a break

You are not a robot, right? You have to take small breaks from your work.

I prefer following the Pomodoro technique, which says that you work for 25 mins, have a laser-sharp focus, and then take 5–7 mins of break. Then again you continue this cycle again and again. This is a very effective technique that you can follow as well to take breaks from your heavy loads of work.

You can also take small breaks between your work to feel relaxed and productive. Plan trips in a month or so, to feel rejuvenated and get back to work with fresh energy.

FIFTEEN

How to Stop Procrastinating and Become Productive

Do you ever feel as if you can't sit down and work? Is your mind wandering constantly from one thought to another? Well, you're not alone.

Before moving on, I'll give you the solution upfront.

To stop procrastinating, you must eliminate all distractions from your life. As a result, your mind's focus capability- will increase.

Currently, many people scroll on social media for most of their days. Hence they habituate jumping from one piece of information to another.

Thus when they sit down to work, the value of their outcomes- will be inferior than if they had the capability of aiming their undivided attention toward a single goal.

Now, let's discuss distractions and how they harm your productivity.

The fierce power of distractions in our lives

Distractions are all around us. In fact, while reading this story, your mind is likely to wander to other thoughts, such as how many likes you got on your latest post.

Because of that, your ability to focus- is significantly reduced. So, how does this happen?

Let's take social media as an example, as it's the easiest one to demonstrate my argument on.

When you're on social media, it bombasts your mind with tons of data. As a result, you'll get used to jumping from one task to another.

Moreover, your mind will regularly look for the next dopamine rush. Therefore, once you'll want to work, your mind will still jump from one task to another.

Social media, and all distractions, are high-stimulus. As such, they'll provide your brain with enormous amounts of dopamine.

Now, you must understand that work is a low-stimulus action. In that case, your mind will reject work and embrace the next dopamine hit because what's more difficult, concentrating or chilling?

Minimize distractions

To become more productive, minimizing the amount of time you spend distracted- is your next step.

Instead, it'll be best if you embrace the state of being undistracted. As a result, with dedication, your mind will be capable of aiming its undivided attention toward a single task.

Additionally, it won't look for the next dopamine hit, as you won't need it. Because of that, once it occurs, starting to work, which is the hardest part- becomes effortless.

So, let's examine the primary source of distractions for most people. Moreover, I'll demonstrate the #1 step you must take to see developments in your productiveness.

Delete social media

Social media is the primary distraction source for most people, especially young individuals. Because of that, to become more productive, you must cut the distractions in their origin.

First, let me clarify. Although the subheading of this section is "delete social media," you don't have to take this drastic step.

Nonetheless, the less time you spend distracted, the more productive you'll be, as your focus and attention span will improve.

Because of that, you may need to take a step back from social media and minimize your use.

However, I want to emphasize that although you may not be willing to take such a drastic step and delete social media, you can minimize its use.

As a result, you'll still notice results in your productiveness, even if you don't delete it.

Still, to thoroughly develop your productiveness, it'll be best if you delete social media and stop using it altogether.

Final words

Social media is the primary source of distractions in today's world. Hence the more you use it, the less focused you'll be.

For instance, I don't see myself in the same position without having deleted social media 12 months ago.

In fact, I would've never opened my business and never become a writer. Thus I'm more grateful for having deleted all social media platforms from my phone than I can express with words.

SIXTEEN

6 BEST HABITS TO DEVELOP IF YOU WANT TO BE SUCCESSFUL

Good habits can be your shortcut to success

Talent is overrated. Success is all about building good habits and practicing them consistently in all areas of your life.

Of late, there's much hype about cultivating positive habits, and rightly so. The reason's not difficult to figure out, though.

Good habits serve you better and are more reliable than willpower when getting things done and achieving long-term goals.

With empowering habits in place, you don't have to worry about your state of mind or mood. You're in a position to take action at the appropriate time and get things done when they need to be done without your mind or whims playing spoilsport.

Habits, thus, hold the key to your success in life. If you put in the effort and develop good habits, anything is possible. Like Charles Duhigg said, "There's nothing you can't accomplish if you get the habits right."

Here are the six best habits to build and stick around if you want to be insanely successful.

1. Audit your time

Time is the most precious resource that you have, but most people don't realize it. All they do is complain about how time flies past each day and they're not able to do what they plan to.

Doing work effectively and productively is critical for success in all areas of life. To get more control over your time, you must know where your time goes daily. For this, get into the habit of tracking your time. People who work at their peak level of productivity regularly engage in monitoring their time closely and actively looking for time drains.

Audit your time by tracking how you spend your day and note where your get carried away and lose sense of time. Be honest with yourself and record every hour of your waking time.

Recording time over several days or weeks will provide sufficient data, which you can then sit down and analyze. Going through the numbers of the log will give you valuable information and provide you with a clear idea of your time drains.

Once you understand where and how you're wasting time, you'll be able to plug the loopholes, avoid frittering away time, plan better, and schedule tasks mindfully.

Saving your precious time will increase productivity, keep stress at bay and help maintain a proper work-life balance. You'll also be able to spend quality time with your loved ones, carve out me-time and do things you love.

2. Work through your problems

Problems are an integral part of anyone's life. They are stressful because they obstruct the smooth working of your life and jeopardize your plans or threaten to stall your progress.

Simply put, problems are undesirable situations or conditions that are difficult to deal with and prevent you from carrying out your day-to-day tasks effectively.

While fixing problems is challenging, and many ignore or try to dodge their problems, not sorting them out and clearing the obstacles out of your way poses even greater challenges.

Lingering problems can be a source of great distress. Therefore, whether they are work-related or personal issues, get into the habit of addressing them as soon as you identify them.

Dealing with any problem is not as difficult as people make it out to be. As with most other things, there's a method to it. Problem-solving is indeed a skill that you must master if you want to succeed in life.

Most problems, including the complicated ones, can be easily broken down into smaller parts and dealt with piecemeal.

Your ability to find solutions, figure your way out through perplexing situations, and fix the mess you find yourself in will serve you throughout and help you better your life.

3. Pay attention to small things

Most of your precious time is wasted when you are lost in thoughts and work with a wandering mind.

When you're zoned out, you operate on autopilot mode and do things mechanically without being aware of them. You are detached from your surroundings and go with the flow.

Such a mental state may be helpful when you're engaged in a creative pursuit or solving a problem. However, in this spaced-out state, you just go through the motions without really thinking about what you are doing. Hence, you cannot expect to do quality work or learn new things.

There are several reasons for low attention span, ranging from physical exhaustion to mental stress to emotional overwhelm and sleep deprivation. Finding and removing the underlying causes that steal your attention can help you focus better on your work and unburden your mind.

To zone in and pay attention to small things, build the habit of examining closely the process you are involved in and the steps you are taking.

Make conscious efforts to pay attention to what you are doing, why you are doing it, and the outcome of the efforts you are expecting. This will drastically boost your productivity and reduce your chances of making mistakes.

Eliminating the clutter, creating a minimalist environment, and working in a distraction-free space can help you a lot in being attentive while working.

4. Dismiss negative thoughts

The pursuit of success involves facing difficulties and enduring many challenges. You also have to deal with the naysayers who laugh at your goals and demoralize you by calling them pipe dreams.

However, the worst enemy lies within you. Negative thoughts and the non-stop inner chatter create feelings of doubt and make you anxious. Any time you allow them to overpower you, the disempowering thought process can take control over you, shake your confidence, and stop you in your tracks.

If you are serious about achieving your goals, develop the habit of combing your thoughts. Be mindful of your inner dialogue, and red flag all the negative thoughts that cross your mind.

Regular practice of the habit of thought processing, separating the chaff from the grain, and dismissing negative thoughts will enable you to adopt a positive mindset and help you march forward boldly towards your goals.

5. Fix the excuses

To accomplish goals and reach great heights, you need to put in the work and follow through. However, if your mind is not wired to go the hard way, it will offer resistance by making random excuses of all kinds.

Excusing yourself from doing something or taking action by telling yourself false stories is your way of avoiding immediate pain and effort but costs you dearly in the long run.

To avoid following the path of least resistance, build the habit of catching yourself when you have an urge to make an excuse.

Examine what action you need to take and the excuses and justifications your mind is pushing your way. This will help you figure out the space from where the excuse is originating.

Many times you're unsure of what needs to be done, how to do it or where to start. Lack of clarity breeds disinterest and pushes you to come up with excuses. You might also offer an excuse because you're tired or bored. A few times, excuses pop up when your actions are not aligned with your values or what you stand for.

Singling out the cause and talking yourself out of lethargy by weighing the pros and cons and reminding yourself of the benefits of taking action will go a long way in beating the negative habit of making excuses.

6. Develop big picture thinking

Too often, people get into the nitty-gritty of things and lose sight of the whole. It's good to be detail-oriented but knowing what is the context of the matter, where you are headed, what is the outcome you are targeting is equally important.

Delving too deep into the minor details can distract your focus from what's essential for the desired outcome to paying very close attention to small things, thus sidestepping you.

Highly successful people train themselves to see life in its entirety and never lose sight of the big picture.

To see how your present actions fit into the grand scheme of things, you must step back, give up the myopic view and think long term.

Your life is not divided into watertight compartments. One sphere of personal or work life causes ripples in other areas as well and so there's a need to cultivate the habit of viewing the bigger picture.

Becoming a big picture person can be of huge benefit to you. You will become more mindful of your choices and decisions, and how they will affect the course of your life. Also, keeping in mind your long-term goals and the results you want will help you bypass the frustration of growing slowly or encountering rough patches.

In Conclusion

Simple every day habits can drastically improve your life. No one knows the importance of positive habits better than the uber successful people who have leveraged their daily habits and routines to accomplish their big goals, which wouldn't have been otherwise possible.

When you build good habits, you automatically do things that must be done when they must be done, irrespective of your mood, motivation, or state of mind. Habits, therefore, ensure each day is a productive day, and you take action and make some progress towards your goals.

SEVENTEEN

WHAT IS MORE IMPORTANT: TIME, MONEY, OR HEALTH?

Time, money, or health — which is more crucial?

Typically, we don't pay attention to all of them at once. Which is the most significant? Whether consciously or unconsciously, we choose one and build our lives around it.

We have the luxury of choosing, the most significant, thus the discussion is now in progress.

Let's first look at each element separately!

Do Share your feedback in the comments below. And share this article with all you love, if you found value! Let's together grow and develop!

Let's examine the first element of "health".

Most people will state that this is the most significant when questioned. Several rituals and exercises that are created expressly for the benefit of the physical body are implemented when one chooses health.

Fortunately, the emotional and intellectual elements of the body can also benefit from maintaining optimal bodily balance.

Let's now discuss "wealth".

This term gives the user a variety of possibilities. Around the world, people pursue financial success to extremes.

Without money, and our terrible living situations may undoubtedly make us suffer, as well as the emotional and cerebral components, from a persistent lack of fresh and nourishing meals, which will also shorten our time.

Let's now discuss "time."

We all receive time equally, which makes it special.

True, some stay longer than others, but I'm talking about how much time each of us gets while we're here. The distribution of the 24 hours in a day is equally available to everyone, and it is freely provided to all facets of life, whether they are human or animal.

Perception may navigate time.

Do we have enough time to tidy the home before your mother arrives for supper and still make it to the game? I simply don't have the time to write the book between my career and studying. I have lots of time to finish high school, but I want to travel through Europe in a backpack first.

Suppose we run out of time. I believe it is acceptable to state that, under our current knowledge, there is no us if there is no time. Our existence cannot exist without time. From our vantage point, time and life are inextricably linked, and neither exists without the other.

Can we live without being healthy? Yes. Although it would be sad and brief, we can live without health.

Can we live without money? Yes. We all do, a lot of us.

However, life is impossible without time. Time is thus of utmost importance. We have life when we have time.

The truth is that money and health are nothing without time.

The most crucial factor is time, yet it is too frequently ignored.

We tend to undervalue and underestimate the importance of time because we have the impression that it is an unending resource.

The quote "live each day as if it were your last" is one you've probably heard.

You begin to appreciate some of life's basic pleasures more when you are aware of how little time you have left. You don't take the time to stop and smell the roses as much when you believe you have a lifetime ahead of you.

Until the well runs empty, we are unaware of the value of water. The same may be said about time.

You may be wondering what this has to do with my money. Your finances are important to the situation.

Having the means to pay for the activities you wish to perform with your time makes them possible. Even if your only goal is to spend time with your family, you will still need money to fund your expenses while not working.

Your money serves as the fuel for your retirement goals, much like petrol keeps a car moving.

For a variety of reasons, your health is also very important. Many of the insurances you could desire or need are health-based. The likelihood of being approved at a lower cost increases with improved health.

You could be compelled to leave your job at an awkward moment if your health deteriorates.

The choice is a part of life.

We all play games with our riches, our health, and our free time. We have an option. Every choice we make is based on one of these categories, and how we spend our time will ultimately decide both our health and our riches.

Time gives us the opportunity to pursue health to the desired level and to acquire money of all kinds and amounts.

May each of our decisions take the form of elegant brushstrokes that are infused with the color that time has bestowed. I believe time will lead.

EIGHTEEN

HATE YOUR CURRENT LIFE? START WAKING UP EARLY

It's Sunday night and you are scrolling through pictures of how rad your weekend has been, or you slept through the entire 48 hours and are contemplating how perfect it would have been if only you could do this all seven days a week.

Your body doesn't really need that much sleep, or that crazy level of partying. However, what it is craving is something you love as much, and feel that positive towards and excited about.

This is not me typing randomly created scenarios, because I speak from personal experience. I spent over a year staying awake till late with Netflix and Prime Video to accompany me on days when whichever boyfriend I had in my life could not speak to me for hours at end. This would be followed by me waking up at an hour that would leave me with only five minutes to wash and change and rush to work to only be late by half an hour if not more. My alarms would start ringing from six or seven am, but the first one I would hear would be the one at 8:55 AM after which I would snooze twice and finally jump out of bed at 9:05. And this was on a good day.

When your routine involves rushing straight to work, doing actual work on some days and immersing yourself in busywork on others, coming back home to eat food and befriend OTT content websites, you really don't have much to genuinely be excited about or look forward to. Even though I believed that humans are meant to create and not just consume blindly, not much creation can happen when your life is not just mechanical, but so deprived of growth in any form. Plus, even if you are only going to consume content, it has to be better than being updated on the latest episode of House of Cards/ Broklyn Nine Nine/ Insert Your Favourite Show.

If you are not the biggest fan of your job, the situation is only getting worse. You might not realise it now, but the clock is ticking and your mind is the iron that is rusting, or the plant whose leaves are slowly turning yellow, and will soon dry out and before you know it, they will all fall off. You want to be a well nurtured plant, the kind you'd want to keep on your side table, your kitchen cabinet or inside your living room.

Why wake up early though, what does that have to do with any of this?

Kickstarting your day the right way does not happen with a magic potion that can be gulped down to magically teach you the nuances of it. However, the way your day commences has a direct impact on how you will be feeling about yourself through the day, at least the first half if not the entire day.

Advocates of the 5 AM Club would hand you a list with a dozen items to include in your morning routine. Let's be a little honest and slightly practical though — which person who has struggle with sleeping on time and waking up before they REALLY have to else they'd lose their job, would ever manage to wake up at 5 AM to do a million things, or even one for that matter?

The only running I did in my life was the one each morning to catch the Metro, right from college days to my initial months at work. Today, if I decide to go for a 10K run the next morning, I know I can. These things never happen overnight, so be patient with yourself and be kind to yourself.

Your mornings need a structure, which comes with doing one thing you choose, that you would actually like to have ticked off your checklist, and do it right after waking up. It could include exercising (which is never a bad idea), reading, writing, meditating or even making yourself some breakfast. The key is that it should either enrich your mind or strengthen your body. If either of these things are focused on, right at the beginning of the day, your day has started on a successful note and you can pass that feeling on to other tasks that you do as well.

Do this for 15 minutes, if that is all you can give to begin with. Instead of 9 AM, try waking up at 8:45 and walk around a bit. Do this for a week. Shift it to 8:30 the next week. It will seem easier. Slowly, you'd have enough time to do three things in the morning and that's before your work day even starts. Soon enough, you'd want to have a list of tasks to do for yourself in the evening too, which most likely won't even involve Netflix because you'd be so consumed by growing and hustling that you'd struggle to find time for bothering about who married whom and who's going to die in all the Series you once used to follow religiously.

Have a strong what and why, and keep at it. Start small, grow slow and remain consistent.

My whats and whys:

I workout because it keeps me fit, which makes me feel stronger. It also keeps my mood in check and gives me a sense of accomplishment right when I start the day. (Read this to understand how you can be fitter too, this year)

I read because it gives me material to think about. It helps me learn from people who are experts in their respective field and I can capture years of what they have studied in 300 pages.

I journal each night because it is a good way to reflect on my day and decipher what's bothering me, if there is anything, and analyse and solve it. It helps me document my life. In this way, I also understand how things I spent a lot of energy on a few weeks back don't bother me anymore which makes me not waste my time on issues like that now when I come across them.

We need to feel in control of our lives.

There are circumstances where we are stuck at a particular place and at that given point in time, there are factors that disable us from getting out of it. Of course I wish every human had the freedom to be able to say 'No' to things they didn't like, but in the practical world, that hardly exists.

Your job takes $1/3^{rd}$ of your day, and if you include your commute time, you might stretch it to 1/2 of your day, although it's up to you to consider your commute time part of your work or not. I utilise mine for reading or listening to audiobooks so it's actually a good way to utilise that one hour of my day.

The remainder of your day is your empty canvas — fill it with colours of your choice.

You need to have things to look forward to, and the fact that you have something you probably aren't too fond of (aka your current life), should give you enough motivation to find things that you would like or would help you grow in a way or two.

From the night owl who used to drag her half drowsy ass to work each morning and cry through it all, I managed to make myself a person who has a structure to every hour for her day both pre & post work hours. No, it is not a time table. It's a list of things out of which some I love, and some I have to learn to love, but through each, I ensure that I grow.

NINETEEN

FIVE EPIC MISTAKES PEOPLE MAKE WHEN TRYING TO ACHIEVE THEIR DREAMS

There are way more than five epic mistakes people typically make when trying to achieve their dreams but for today, I'll focus on five biggies.

1. We give up before we reach success.

As humans we tend to over-estimate what we can do in the short term and under-estimate what we can do over longer periods of time. As such, we get frustrated when we run into obstacles that slow us down or even stop us in our tracks. Inevitably, the process turns out to be harder than we thought, our goal costs more than we anticipated and we don't seem to have enough time to move the ball forward.

Here's the thing… most if not all of those events are bound to happen. So here's the secret; make sure you are absolutely passionate about your goal because if you're not, you'll give up before you reach success. In other words, follow your passion.

2. We procrastinate.

Who doesn't procrastinate, right? I'm guilty of it myself. But there are ways to get past that. One thing I tend to do (and recommend) is to schedule time for my future. I schedule about three hours a day to sit in front of my computer and "work". Yes, I'm sorry, getting where you want to go does take work, or effort, or energy. Whatever you want to call it, if you want to create the life of your dreams, you're going to have to spend time working on it.

Now, this is where what I discussed before come in... your passion. If you are passionate about what you're doing and the goal your after, it won't be work. You could be saying, I don't have three hours a day to work on it. That's fine. Find an amount time that works for you. It may require you to get up an hour earlier or spend some of your day off focusing on your desired future but hey, do you want to live your dream life or would you rather procrastinate? So the lesson here is don't procrastinate.

3. We don't believe we can do it.

Our biggest enemy is in our own head. We constantly exercise our limiting beliefs. That's our brain telling us "you can't do it." My mother used to tell me, " Can't never did anything." She was, and continues to be, correct.

We also lack self-confidence. At times we don't feel we have the c ourage, determination and skills to accomplish our goals. Here's what I say to that... If you don't have the skills, what's stopping your from learning that new skill? Being a lifelong learner is key to success in today's ever-changing world.

I'm pretty sure you have a phone. And that means you have access to all of the world's knowledge right there in the palm of your hand. Use it. Be curious and search for what you need. I'll bet you find it. That will give you confidence. And confidence gives you courage and courage leads to determination. So please, stop doubting yourself. You can do it.

4. We think we don't have the resources.

When we think of resources (or lack thereof), we typically think we don't have enough money, we don't know the right people or we don't have the time. I'm here to tell you all of those are simply problems to be solved.

Over the years I have developed a series of statements that I use to guide me in times of crisis. I call them Rudyisms and I have one that relates to resources. It is as follows, "Where my budget ends, my creativity begins." As that relates to money, ask yourself, how can I adjust my strategy so it doesn't cost so much? As for connections, reach out to people you don't know. Now, I know that requires some self-confidence but we already discussed that. Just do it. Introduce yourself in person or virtually via email, linkedin, facebook or wherever that person resides. If you're passionate about what you're doing (as we discussed), you'll probably make some headway. What's the worse thing that can happen? You'll get a no. And if that happens, just keep on looking. As for time, stop procrastinating and you'll find the time.

5. We are scared of success.

As crazy as that sounds people actually fear success. Success means something will change. And people fear change. I know, crazy right? But true. Here's the thing... what people fear most is actually something we can control. People fear uncertainty. We're uncertain of what happens if... (fill in the blank). So what's the solution? The solution lies in the opposite of uncertainty — which is certainty. Duh. So do what you can to make things more certain. How do we do that? We educate ourselves, we hypothesize, we plan, we prepare. By doing those things, you will have already thought out the possible results and will know and be certain of what is to come so you are not scared of your own success.

There are plenty more mistakes to discuss but for now, let's stick with that. Thank you for choosing to spend your time and attention with me. I hope my sharing this little secret with you makes your day a little brighter and helps you move toward the life of your dreams.

TWENTY

How Clarity and Confidence can help you overcome Procrastination

Procrastination can be a big problem in many aspects of our lives. It can be challenging to get work done, it can make it hard-tackling chores around the house and when we have so many things that need to be done, procrastination can cause a lot of stress. In this article, I will tell you about two strategies that if used together, will help you overcome procrastination and get more out of your day.

Many people struggle with procrastination, but what if it's more than just laziness?

Many people struggle with procrastination, but what if it's more than just laziness?

Procrastination is a symptom of something deeper. If you're not sure what to do or where to start with your goals, it's easy to get caught up in the details and lose sight of the big picture. If this sounds familiar, procrastination may be a sign that you need clarity around your purpose and values. Clarity is essential for confidence. In order to move forward confidently towards our goals, we need clarity around the why behind our actions — why we want them in the first place, why they matter and what we're willing to sacrifice along the way.

Whether it's working on an important project or making time for exercise at home after work each day (or both), living a healthy lifestyle requires us to take action towards our desired results each day. However, when we don't know what those results should look like or how long it will take us to get there, taking action becomes difficult if not impossible!

Clarity and Confidence are often the missing links.

Clarity and confidence are often the missing links. Clarity is about knowing what you want and why you want it. Confidence is about believing that you can achieve it. They're two separate things, but they go hand in hand: if you don't know what it is that you want, how can you ever be confident in achieving it? Of course, some people may lack clarity because they feel stuck in a rut or don't know where to start. Other times, though, we know exactly what we want but feel as though our dreams are out of reach or too difficult for us to achieve on our own (or with limited resources).

When you know what you want to achieve and why it's easier to go after it.

You're not alone. Procrastination is a complex problem that usually has many causes and solutions. But first, you need to understand what's holding you back from moving forward with your goals. Here are some questions to ask yourself:

Do I know my motivation? Why do I want this? What would happen if I didn't get it? What would happen if I did get it (and why would that be good)?

Do I know my goal? What are the key steps between where I am right now and where I want to be in terms of achieving this goal? Can I break it down into smaller pieces that are easier to tackle one at a time, or will taking action now make things worse later on when it's harder than ever before?

Do I know my resources: how much money do I have available, how much time do I have available -what skills and tools are available too; what knowledge does someone else have which can support me in getting closer to my goal; who might help me reach my goal faster because they've already done something similar before -what opportunities exist for funding or other forms of support etcetera...

Confidence in your abilities and the belief that you can do it helps too.

Confidence is a feeling we have about ourselves. Confidence is not a feeling that we have about our abilities. Confidence is a feeling that we have about our ability to achieve our goals. Confidence isn't a feeling at all; it's based on what you believe and how strongly you believe it, which can be influenced by your past experiences and the quality of those experiences.

It's important to understand that confidence isn't just an idea in your head — it affects how you behave outside of yourself as well. If you think something will be difficult or scary, then it will likely feel like more of an obstacle than if someone else thought it was easy or fun! This means that if your mind is telling you something like "I'm not good at math," then this belief may affect how well (or poorly) perform when taking exams later down the road because those thoughts could become self-fulfilling prophecies over time."

Clarity around your goals is a huge step towards overcoming procrastination but how do you get this?

Clarity around your goals is a huge step towards overcoming procrastination but how do you get this?

In order to achieve clarity, it's important to know what you want to achieve and why. The clearer you are about your goal, the easier it will be for you to reach it. For example, if your goal is "to pay off my debt", then knowing how much debt there is would be very helpful in terms of calculating where exactly on the journey towards paying off those debts that you are currently at.

Having said that, having a clear picture of what needs to happen before we can achieve our goals can also help us get there faster and more easily because we don't waste time trying out different things when there's no point in doing so because they won't take us anywhere near where we're trying hard enough (or at all) go

Steps to creating clarity around your goals.

To begin, identify your goal. There are several different ways to do this:

Take a step back from the situation and ask yourself, "What is the goal that I am trying to achieve?"

Ask someone close to you what they think your true goal is, regardless of whether or not they are aware of your current obstacles preventing the achievement of that goal (this will prevent them from giving advice based on their own experiences). This person may not know why the goal is important to you personally — they may just see it as something that needs doing because everyone else thinks so — but having another perspective can help clarify things further when combined with self-reflection and introspection. Remember: clarity comes first; confidence follows!

Identify and become clear about your goal.

Identify and become clear about your goal.

Before you can stop procrastinating, you need to know what it is that you want. Set aside some time for this exercise and ask yourself: "What do I want?" Then ask yourself again, but in a different way: "How will I know when I have achieved my goal?"

You may find it helpful to write down your answer to these questions. Doing so will help clarify exactly what you're trying to achieve and why — and in turn, provide the basis for creating a more realistic plan of action.

With a clearer sense of direction, it's easier to set milestones along the way (e.g., "I'll start saving $20 per month once my debt reaches $5k"). These smaller benchmarks will help keep things within reach while giving you something tangible to work toward at each step along the road (i.e., "I've saved up enough cash for my trip!"). In addition, defining how long each milestone should take can give an added incentive; if there's no finish line in sight then there's nothing stopping us from getting tired or distracted along the way!

Dig deep into precisely why this goal is meaningful for you; Why does it matter? How will your life be better or different once the goal is achieved?

No matter how much you know about the value of your goal, it's easy to get distracted by other priorities. To help keep yourself on track, dig deep into precisely why this goal is meaningful for you; Why does it matter? How will your life be better or different once the goal is achieved?

Once you have answers to these questions, write them down and review them regularly. This will help keep them fresh in your mind and remind you why achieving this particular goal is important to YOU. It's also OK if other goals are more important than others; just remember that all of our goals add up over time.

Taking time out every day to reflect on our progress towards our long term vision can also help us stay motivated when we hit bumps along the way. Think about what percentage of complete do I feel like I am with my current projects today? How many months are left until my next big milestone? What resources do I need in order to accomplish this task? These are all questions worth asking so that we can look back after each step forward has been taken!

Ask yourself this simple question — "What do I need to reach my desired outcome?" Then list all of the things that come to mind. This might include training programs, nutrition, time management, team members or coaches. These are your resources.

Ask yourself this simple question — "What do I need to reach my desired outcome?" Then list all of the things that come to mind. If you're thinking sports this might include training programs, nutrition, time management, team members or coaches. These are your resources.

If you don't have the resources necessary to achieve a goal then it will be difficult to realize it in reality no matter how clarity and confidence you have. This means you can identify the gaps and start working out how to close them.

Conclusion

We've covered some of the main causes and effects of procrastination, and we've taken a look at some tips for overcoming it. But I don't want to close things off with the idea that these are all hard-and-fast rules. In truth, everyone deals with procrastination differently, and there isn't a one-size-fits-all solution for getting rid of it altogether. The best we can do is learn about ourselves and how we work so that we can make decisions that help us reach our goals in life.

TWENTY-ONE

How To Break Bad Habits & Get Better Everyday

Are you stuck in a rut? Feeling like you can't seem to break your bad habits? It's time to start getting better everyday. Implement these tips and see how you can change your life for the better. You'll be surprised at what you can accomplish.

1. Set realistic goals. When you're trying to break a bad habit, it's important to set achievable goals. If your goal is too lofty, you're more likely to get discouraged and give up. But if your goal is realistic, you'll be more likely to stick with it and see results.

2. Find a support group. There's nothing like knowing that you're not alone in your struggle to break a bad habit. Finding a supportive group of friends or family members can make all the difference. They can provide encouragement and hold you accountable when you start to slip up.

3. Create a plan of action. Once you've set your goals and assembled your support group, it's time to create a plan of action. This plan should include specific steps that you'll take to reach your goals. It should also include a timeline for reaching these goals. Having a plan will help keep you on track and motivated.

4. Be patient. Breaking a bad habit can be a long and difficult process. Don't get discouraged if you don't see results immediately. Just keep working at it and eventually you'll start to see progress.

5. Seek professional help. If you're struggling to break a bad habit on your own, don't be afraid to seek professional help. There are many qualified therapists and counselors who can assist you in overcoming your challenges.

Breaking a bad habit can be tough, but it's not impossible. With a little effort and perseverance, you can make it happen. Just remember to set realistic goals, find a supportive network, and create a plan of action. And most importantly, be patient with yourself. These things take time. But if you stick with it, eventually you'll see results.